ANIMATRON

R.J. Breemer

CONTENTS

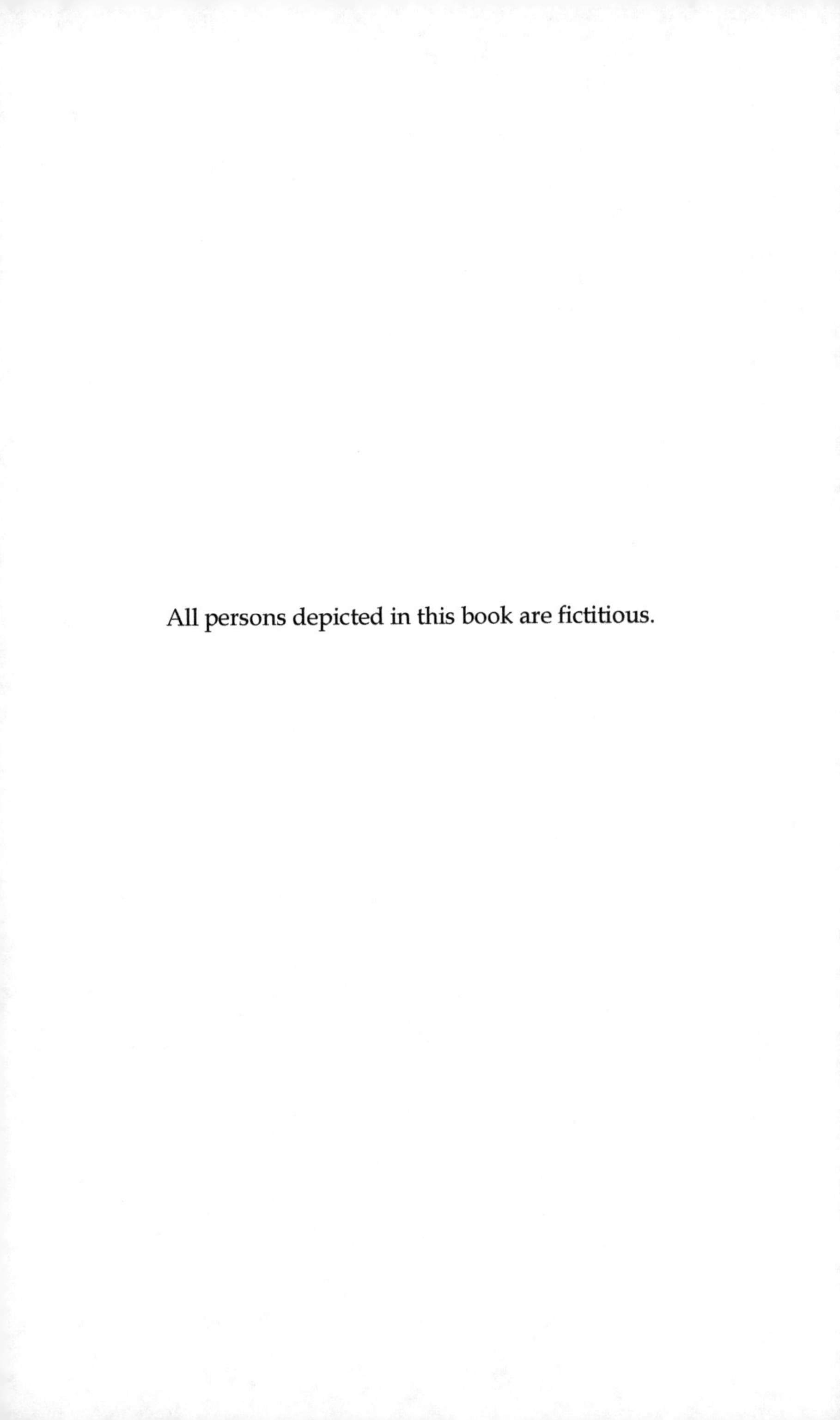
All persons depicted in this book are fictitious.

PROLOGUE

FACTION LIST IN MASTERDOM SERIES mentioned in this book, along with their Primer (humanoid major species);

UNITED WORLDS (Human) – Milky Way.

The second member of Galactic League. When almost wholly conquered by the Neo States at the earth, Felidean comes from space to help, they helped humankind, starting with the giving of super-advanced aerospace technology. Multiethnic mankind's organization was changed to the United Worlds when the space colonies began. They have thousands of colonies from terraformed planet to space station across the Milky Way, with trillions of human populations. Thirteen allies consist of; African Union, Centric Bloc, European Lineage, Kingdoms of Commonwealth, Latin Order, The Outsiders, Pacific Unity, Orient Dynasty, Sinai Ring, Slavic Blood, Southeast Association, Southern Nations, and United of America. A colony can have more than one alliance, while most colonies use two time format; Earth Time or E.T. and their own star system time.

NEO STATES (Neo-Human) – Milky Way.

At the 21st century, humans were divided into two sub-species: Human and Neo-Human. It started from a hidden movement of scientists in the Neogenesis Laboratory — also called "The Dark Lab" — by a secret institution in the development of

Super Genetic Human and was located in Antarctica. The State Company was named Neo State based on the high technology — law of "The Corporation-State," were every person abilities and behavior are recorded with limited privilege. States are ruled by skilled people based on their achievement records and not politic. Neo-humans were created with various experiments with almost no bioethics and born with the best DNA. Similar to Vampires' appearance in myth, they have pale skin, long canines, colorful hair even though most are black, and blue-white eyes that glow especially in the dark, with superior cunning abilities, powerful muscles, and incredible night vision—but that makes their eyes and skin sensitive to light. They live on a strict protein diet of meat and fruit. Their ruler was a brown human named the King, who continued to be cloned with new bodies and immortalize.

GAIGA CLAN AND WATCHER (Felidean) – Milky Way.

The first member of Galactic League. Elders of GaiGa Clan was the most tremendous power in the Milky Way. The Elders at Felidean, consisting of seventy individual Felidean leaders in various star systems, communicate through an inter-space-time technology called Telepathy.

Not like an ordinary Felidean, Elders live almost forever with a strict diet of holy fruits. There were only fifty left because twenty elders had rebelled to become Star Rangers. Felideans are creatures like big cats that have many color races; some are tailed and some are not, shaped like humans with elegant bodies and cute faces. There are giants, human-sized, and dwarf Felidean with big ears. GaiGa have guardians of pure giant noble species from the Milky Way called Marvelan or Marvel, which are Pure-Human, Pure-Kian, Pure-Utan, and more.

CYBER AUTOCRACY or CENTRAL (Android) – Milky Way.

The third member of the Galactic League. This AI nation was created by the collaboration between Felidean and Humans. The Androids are smart as the human brain can achieve. They were independent and pure humanoid machines. They became galaxy guards and were made to specifically fight the Star Ranger. Their main weapon was a cyber attack and robotic engineering. They're all controlled from Central, the main core. With variety of armies like Silver army, Cancri army from the diamond planet, Neon army, etc.

STAR RANGER (Diversified Cyborg of multispecies) – Milky Way.

The machine created by the Elders who rebelled from the Watcher. The rebels are poisoned and live for a short time. They create an automatic factory that manages, makes, and modificate other creatures in the galaxy to become a loyal brainwashed cyborg army, a combination of the best between flesh and machine, with the aim of revenge to the long lifespan Watcher. The Ranger are disciplined by the Mothers. With cyberpunk works, they have much division from STARS—which is a Human cyborg—Wasps—the female's cyborg—Animals cyborg in any size, and many more.

SANCTUARY EMPIRE (Diversified multispecies).

Called as Constellations Empire by Human. Combined with the power that controls between galaxies, they evolved to replace their elders, headed by an Emperor of unknown origin; they came from a combination of galaxies deep in Supercluster to fight Elders, Dragon, Abaddon, and anything that stand in their way. They are the most progressive coalition of various creatures—with different celestial objects and weapons that have never been encountered by humans—built to conquer. Known kingdoms to human are Kingdom of AzuRa (Amphibian of Andromeda), Kingdom of LaZaRa (Reptilian of Triangulum), and Kingdoms of AvEn (Avian a mixed winged-like species of M81 group). They use madness inter-species breed slave's army from captured alien of various planet.

DRAGON (Cursed Seraphim).

Hostile invader or cursed heavener. Also called Merc — pure energy creatures, they can possess other species to become Transgon; their spaceship is called Astrogon. The biggest Dragon is named as corrupted Seraphim or space serpent with the scale from an island to a planet, and can live in stars. They want to banish all sins from the universe, including themselves later. With the aim that after all wage of sins is paid, the Creator will forgive the cursed galaxies.

BLACK STAR (Cursed Abaddon).

Hostile invader or cursed heavener. The cell-evolver force. Their Majestic creatures live in force formed from dead stars or bottomless pit, call themselves as Maker, but others called them Destroyer. They control Grimmer (converted flesh) and Harvester (mixed metal and flesh). They love to deceive the outsider with lust and power. They want to convert all beings to become one with their mind, and finally stop all the sins as they dream, with the aim that the Creator will forgive the cursed galaxies after nobody has sinful thinking aftermath.

DIMENSIONAL KINGDOM (Holy Master of the three realms).

Unimaginable mastery system from Heaven realm, Creator of the World realm — the universe, and Underworld realm — the world with no worlds. The Holy Master control all of the realms by Words which is the Master itself. Cursed the Virgo supercluster that contains all troubled factions because of their free will that turned in chaos and sins. Instead of banishing the sinners completely, the Master let them live as example — so everyone else will learn from the sinners mistakes.

OTHER KNOWN FACTIONS WHICH ARE NOT MENTIONED BUT EXIST.

Other Fallen Angels, LheZer Clan (Humanoid Arthropodan from M101 group), MoMo Clan (Molluscan from M51 group, extinct because of Abaddon invasion), Freedom Fighter/FF (Mixed species race from Milky Way), The Warrior/ Bandit/ Avenger (Mixed alien species from space pirate), other Milky Way humanoid species like; Kian the Skinny wood-like yellow alien, Utan the hairy alien like ape, Pigin the big pig-like alien, Gnomen an ugly dwarf alien, and much more.

CHAPTER 1

An order is received for a package to be delivered. But the package must be carried to a forbidden planet called the Apen — far away, a world that was once the best human colonies from the ES Alliance.

On a quiet day on planet Nova Anglia, which is one of the colonies of the Kingdoms of the Commonwealth faction, Marco "Polo" Domingo was lying on the couch, relaxed while looking at the white computer screen in the lightness of his working room. When the e-mail came in, he immediately sat straight up while looking at the source of the sound; the e-mail was sent from a nearby robot factory.

Marco got up and read the contents of the message: "Attention, need a reliable package sender who braves enough for inter-planetary travel and will be paid dearly. If interested, come and meet directly in our office. No phone or mail. Will be paid as much as five billion gold coins credits."

He leaned for a moment on the chair and thought about the offer. He then rushed to meet his friend who was downstairs; as he descended the stairs, he saw Hendrik sitting while thinking.

Marco said to him "Hey, amigo, there is a special order at a high price; I got it from our email. They ask us to meet in their office if we're interested."

Hendrik looked slowly at him, and then answered, "Oh bollocks. Meet them? Why not just come directly to us? It seems like they have been rejected everywhere or might just be nonsense, or scam."

Marco said "The address is accredited, came from special net-line and it can't be a scam. Are you sure no one is calling us?"

Then their boss—Franky—came and broke down the door of the room and entered with an angry face. Franky said, "Bloody hell! Debt collector came this morning. They asked for payment with interest, but we lack orders, and I can't pay them!"

Before Franky finished speaking, Hendrik said, "Hey, boss, so don't get drunk and lose too much gambling. Ha ha ha ha."

Hearing that, Franky was very angry and started to slap him, but Marco was blocking him. Indeed, their salary was also not paid; Franky, their boss, also had a debt to his employees.

"Calm down, boss, we got an offer!" Marco yelled at Franky.

"Offer? All right, don't shout; I'm almost deaf. Jump to the point, how much is the payment?" asked Franky as he quieted his emotions.

"Five billion gold coin credits," Marco answered.

Franky became excited, but Hendrik was just silent—not believing—with his mocking laughter.

"Where is the package? Is there a down payment?" Franky asked excitedly.

"No" Marco replied, "I mean not yet, we have to meet them."

Immediately Franky ordered him into the car, and both went to the address. They passed the night city, with mass tall buildings with the shape of a box and filled by underpass. Nova Anglia was a little bit cold, but the city has the shape of classic European buildings merged with futuristic architecture with lots of beautiful light, and dark tunnel. A big, amazing river divided the night city; their street lamps are very traditional. Their people dress in art mixed with future tech, which leads to the world of true modernization between cultural heritage and space-age—like most colonies. People there use flying motors and fast trains, but mostly wheeled vehicles. A future where everyone dreamed to live—a place full of automatize, free knowledge, innovation, luxury, and rapid technology. The address of the place was not too far away, and when they got there, they saw a large manufacturer owned by an independent, smart Android Robot nation called Cyber Autocracy, or also known as Central. On the inside there was not a single human; there were many strong robot guards inside. They allowed the two men to enter and directed them into a particular room.

* * *

An Android person named Ariana 65 came in; she looked like a human, but had a body of a silver machine. Her metal skin sparks the light reflection with the shape of a woman. They look similar to silver humans, like most Central Androids. They have different helmet shapes on their heads that look like a mixture of animals, but in the coolest way. Ariana with her bright white spectacles and beautiful humanoid face greet them in calm voices. She said, "Greetings human. Please sit down. My name is Ariana."

Franky said, "It's a pleasure to meet you, my name is . . . "

She cut him and said "I know who you are. I heard from the officer that you intend to deliver our package—is that right?"

"That's right, my andro lady; one hundred scores for you! I never heard of female Silver Army; I though they're all genderless, you're such a beautiful creation." Franky answered enthusiastically.

"I see your point. Just like those robots, sometimes an android like me where created with extra purpose," she said.

"What, extra purpose?" Asked Franky.

Ignored his question, she continued, "I think you know the

risk because it suits the payment. We want the package to be delivered to planet Apen. Don't worry, you will obtain the best spacecraft from Central for your journey, and be tightly guarded under me."

"Under you? Tight like thigh? Under you thickly tight thigh? Sure, sure, I want that," Franky replied.

With seductive look, she said, "You're such a dirty man, I would love to you clean every part of your dirty body."

Marco became paranoid and asked, "Excuse me, sorry, about the package, then why don't you take it yourself?"

Franky grabbed Marco's mouth and said, "Oh, shut up. Of course, because it is our work."

The Android continued "Our army were banned there by Galactic League current policy. The place is in conflict and quarantined. Only non-faction and neutral people are allowed to enter but at their own risk."

Franky just thought about the money and said, "Calm down, robot lady! Delivering packages even in the war zone I often do! It's even riskier than this, after all. Your payment is worth it like no other—another payment is poor. Is there an upfront payment?"

When a thirst of money darkens his eyes, a man only thinks of himself; that's happened to Franky's mind, where many of his dreams came to appear in his head—a mind not enough gratitude. Not like another project that leads to tons of papers, this one seems simple.

"Signatures First and upfront payment will go into your office account in the amount of ten percent of the total payment," replied the Android.

Franky was pleased to hear that; he signed the contract and thought, *Incredible, a signature and all my debts disappeared.*

The two then returned. Franky devised a plan to throw a party, but before that he wanted to prepare for the party. He began to invite many of his friends. Arriving at the office, they met two other employees, namely Hendrik and Monica.

Monica said "Wait, boss, you suddenly throw a party and pay us three times. Will we be fired?"

Franky laughed wide. He said "No, have fun, all of you get paid because we got a new job! We will go next week, to a new planet."

Hearing that, Hendrik became worried and said "Hey, boss, why not just send a drone or robot there? Why does it have to be everyone? Me, too?"

Holding Hendrik's shoulder, Franky said "Everything must go well, so everyone must come. This is a big project with expensive fees. Yes, Hendrik, you too, my most diligent man. If you don't join, you don't get paid! You lazy bastard."

That night there were many invited guests; seems like everyone is always ready to party in the night city of New Elizabeth — the office was even closed for the time. Many drinks and food were provided. Everything was made expensive, with many drinks and foods from variety of goods across the galaxy. They all danced and had fun. When the party ended, they all slept on their own room. For the next week, they began to prepare everything they needed. Franky began recruiting additional people and robots. The trip was not long, because the distance between the star-planet Apen system and their planet was not too far away. When everything was ready, Franky and his team arrived at the spaceport.

"Marco! I haven't seen you for days, where have you been? Looking for your parents? Oh, my mum made biscuits; they're not very good," Hendrik said.

"Days? I only slept for one night" Marco answered confused.

Franky then came to greet them.

Franky then gave the name of his new team: The Chicken. Laughing and saying, "The name of this team is officially The

Chicken! Because after being fried in misery, we will get delicious chicken meat. Hah! Brilliant right?"

They got a pretty futuristic and large space ship. The team also bought new equipment, cars, weapons, and several small planes and stored them inside the ship.

One of the crew, Monica, began to meet Franky and warned him, "Boss, there is nothing I get."

"Get what? Speak clearly," said Franky.

She answered, "There isn't any news or information about the planet Apen colony and its territories. It all just disappeared from The Net—something was hidden."

"They are in war again," Franky replied irritably. "After all, this is not our business. We only carry packages. You know, the last time we heard years ago, there was a war between the United Worlds—which was a human faction—and a Star Ranger who attacked the Apen colonies. No need to worry; I'm old enough to go through things like this anyway. Stay with me; we will be fine. Long time ago, my ancestors came from Apen colonies, so I am really exciting."

* * *

Then when everything was ready to go, all goods had been transported. Ariana, who is Android Central, came to see that he was carrying some Silver Army, which was also an army version of Android. In space, the silver army dealt with space situations, their silver metallic skin glowing with the light reflection, like stars that are visible in space at night, a true cosmos being. The reflection of their skin made the chart of stars and moon glow like a glass ocean.

Marco asked Franky "Why are there no UW soldiers? Are we not all humans?"

Franky got angry again and answered, "Never mind, you

guys, don't worry. This is between Central and us; why should the UW government participate too, unnecessarily. We are quite legal and official with Central. They are also the closest human alliance against Star Ranger. So shut up and just come along!"

Ariana arrived and said, "This is your ship; we also follow, but from behind. When we reach the planet, we will meet guards outside the planet. They will allow only you to enter, so we just deliver and watch over you. Understood?"

"I'm ready boss!" Franky replied to her. Seeing that Hendrik was standing near, he said with a tired face, "Oh, so she's the boss of my boss, yeah."

Franky brought about fifty people besides his men from his office. They were mercenaries, engineers, scientists, explorers, and some other laborers. With those, Franky made a pretty good personal company—a delivery service company team called The Chicken. Franky also planned to build a more prominent company when he got home.

When all were filled, including a small box which was a package, everything then departed from their planet. Contracted with the same goal, which was only delivering packages.

"Planet Apen, here we come!" said a pilot of the ship.

Their spacecraft was powered by reliable energy-force power, a revolutionary technology that was only used by costly high-end ships, which were faster through light; with the help of artificial space markers and stars, they could determine navigation. The trip took several months, although the planet was not too far away. Their ship was only three hundred meters long, sixty meters wide and not too fast. Space travel—dreams of humans since ancient times—had now become ordinary traffic for the galaxy's most powerful species; like birds in the sky, the man-made ecosystem made its own journeys and brought back stories every time to be told to people who stayed on the planets, watching the sky.

They pass through electromagnetic vacuum and spooky void that makes dizziness with vomiting; some bad weather from space, but everything is still fine. Inside their Starjet The Chicken. Several programs and games had been made so the crew wouldn't get bored. There were also many entertainment venues such as a gym and a place to relax. During their trip they were relaxing; without other jobs besides checking the engine, Franky spent his time drinking with his crew. Marco and Hendrik just wasted time playing video games and watching movies with Monica. Their ship was followed by three Central ships headed by Ariana.

One day, while Marco was jogging down the aisle of the ship, he met a woman who was a scientist—busy in the clinic room. Marco fell in love and wanted to meet her.

"Hi, what are you doing?" Greeted Marco.

Answered the woman, "Hi, sir. I am counting the amount of medicine that I feel is lacking."

"What's your name?" Marco asked.

She replied, "Erica sir, how can I help you?"

Marco took the opportunity and said, "Yes, can you help me with dinner?"

"Sorry, sir," said Erica "I already have a boyfriend; he is on this ship, too; he is a mercenary pilot."

"Oh, sorry, too; at least I tried it, right? Forget about our conversation; happy to work." Marco felt embarrassed and left.

Marco then sat down and told Hendrik when they were eating. Hendrik said, "How sad you are; you should join me in having fun with many women with our short lives. Besides, we still have Monica—why don't you just take her? Hurry up, who knows if we probably will die on the planet Apen."

Then the next day according to the hour on the ship. Marco dressed neatly and met Monica. He found Monica playing in the Gym. His heart brave, he approached the other to tell his feeling, a story where every human must pass—a story of love, or rejection.

"Hi," Marco said.

Monica looked at him. Feeling something strange, she asked, "What's with your weird face? Don't say you will take me out—I'm not interested."

Marco continued, "Come on, at least just as a friend? I never knew that you were beautiful. You know you look beautiful with any clothes . . . "

Before Marco finished speaking, Hendrik entered and said, "Beautiful with anything, especially more so with no clothes."

Hearing Hendrik taunting himself, Marco became embarrassed and left there and said to Hendrik "What are you doing? Don't break my seduction moment! What a jerk."

Hendrik just laughed, feeling funny and said "What a wanker".

* * *

The journey was almost over, and the star system of the Apen Planet was sighted. Franky started talking to Ariana at a meeting, "My Lady Boss, tell me where the country package will be delivered, and how should we do it?"

Ariana replied, "There is a UW headquarters on a neighboring red satellite moon called Luna EL67. They control a space station near the planet Apen. I will go there asking permission while you just go to New Paris City which is the Nation's capital of Grandeville; the big city has the architecture from the Middle Ages to the 22nd Century of the earth. Search and meet someone named Alexa Esprit. She is from the UW resistant group of Grande who are fighting against an army named STARS from Star Ranger—STARS is a special forces that is mostly cyborg. She needs the package; bring it to her in any way, sooner, and try to have your representatives arrive safely. This is the address."

"Good, boss!" Franky said confidently.

After the discussion, the meeting was over, and Franky came out of the hologram meeting room. Monica was standing there asking "What are you talking about, boss? We also need meetings for fellow crew members."

"Take it easy" replied Franky "You will do what must be done."

CHAPTER 2

Monica went to meet Hendrik and Marco because she was still worried. She found they were busy watching a small cinema.

Monica said "Hey, you guys, this might end badly—right? At least let's take time together before we enter the battlefield,"

The woman invited them to relax to drink and eat together in the ship's canteen, but Marco ignored it because he still felt annoyed at being rejected by Monica. With indifferent eyes, Marco only looked toward the TV, and pretended like he was a busy man, but he really was watching everywhere.

Hendrik stood up from his seat and said, "Well, My lady, let's go!"

Marco becomes jealous when the two leave. Arriving there, Monica and Hendrik sat at a round table. Then Marco sauntered and peeked at them in the canteen.

Hendrik said "Monica, you know that Marco likes you, right? I feel guilty for messing with him yesterday."

Monica's face turned red—feeling embarrassed—and said, "Oh, be a little professional; we'll be a work partner. Look, there's a war on the planet. We must be careful—don't be too confident. Our boss Franky is too stupid and hurried."

Then Marco appeared and sat down between the two at one of the chairs. He said to Monica, "Miss, forgive me for being too silly. I am just afraid that I will die too soon—we will pass the battlefield. So I just want, ah . . . forget it."

Monica said to them, "Look, we have been together for a year in this old company. I already consider you as brothers."

Marco sulked and said, "Heh, but I like you!"

Hendrik saw both of them and laughed heartily again.

"No, Marco," said Monica. "I know your dirty mind; you think you can die so your mind is in chaos. I suggest you play in the bathroom."

"But I'm serious about you, Monica!" Marco said, making people around see them. "I don't want to die there without a lover; if indeed we survive, I will marry . . . "

Monica cut Marco's conversation and said, "Enough! If you're really serious, then show it through actions and not words. Then I will be serious. I will doubt you all, and include our boss."

Hendrik then said, "Marco, forget it, you will go home with a lot of money — you can get any woman you want."

Franky comes and says, "Hey kids, what are you doing? Let's take a photo with the update."

The four people then took a photo; the photo was then glued and shared with all of them.

Franky said again, while joking, "Just keep it if later someone asks to retire after returning home."

After they parted ways, Hendrik said to Marco, "Hey, friend, don't be too hasty; play this smoothly."

Feeling too severe and determined, Marco went looking for flowers, and whatever he could use to attract Monica because Hendrik had influenced his mind; he doesn't realize that Hendrik is playing with them.

Seeing Marco's behavior which began to be childish, Hendrik suggested to Monica, "Look, if you really aren't interested in him, then just say so. Don't waste His time." Then Hendrik got out and left her alone.

During that night, Marco almost did not sleep, for looking for flowers and writing love letters. His mind was in a mess for fear that tomorrow he would die while others remained relaxed, just like what Hendrik wanted. Hendrik was playing with his friends; he knows it could hurt, but a human can be evil without even realizing it, especially when it was ignored.

* * *

From outside, Apen Planet has been seen. The planet looks like the earth — but less sea, more land, and the mountain seems dark from space like it has been burned. The planet also has a red moon because of the geology of the satellite that is like the planet Mars. Big clouds and lightning that always indicate storms on Apen. Ariana then turned her ship to that red moon called Luna EL67 to ask permission from the authority; she will visit the UW Headquarters while Franky's ship was still waiting in the atmosphere.

Ariana entered the Luna EL67 which is the moon or the satellite of the Apen planet in the star system. Although it looked empty, Ariana landed the plane at the near visible UW moon base.

The spaceship pilot said, "The Central Ship with code 888 requests permission to enter the landing of the UW moon base at Luna EL67. Waiting for a reply."

As there was no immediate reply, Ariana said, "Don't wait for a reply; land our ship."

The ship then landed at Luna EL67 moon base. It seemed uninhabited as they saw broken glass and unopened gates. They could not see any human or robot there.

The ship pilot asked Ariana about the landing because that place was empty. Ariana answered, "No need to wait for my word." Ariana then called Franky and said "Ariana here to

Frank, the captain of The Chicken. You are allowed to enter by the highest military authority. Please proceed with the delivery."

Hearing Ariana's orders over the phone that allowed him to enter carrying the package to Apen, with enthusiasm, Franky ordered the crew of his ship, "All right, people; it's time. Send pilots and surveillance drones' we'll wait here to see a safe place to go to the target location where the package will be delivered."

After turning off the phone, the Android pilot reacted, "Ariana, I didn't hear that we got permission from anyone."

Ariana replied to the pilot, "We are the highest military authority here; you must be a new pilot who knows nothing. Let the humans enter — they are paid to carry packages."

"What about us?" Asked the pilot.

Ariana replied to him "We are not allowed by Central, only humans, only living beings. We will follow them later."

Monica was a spacejet pilot. When she was about to board her plane, Marco chased and gave a flower. He said, "Come back; forget what happened last night. Think of this flower as a friend's interest, and it doesn't mean anything to me."

Monica received the big flower with a smile and entered her personal spacejet painted in various blues and yellows. With a feeling of satisfaction, a burned relation felt like water that extinguished the fires. A woman and a man related to each in his or her own unique way. A man that hides his feelings is like a woman who hates to express her emotions.

Ten Franky spacejets were sent close to the surface of Apen — ten small camera drones joined together. From the results of the ship's sensors, there were many hot spots or fire and a little electricity in various regions.

"Look at it, boss," Hendrik said as the ship operator. "It seems like there's shit tons of fighting happening below; it can be seen from the sensor that only a few urban regions still have electricity. This place seems to have just been wholly burned by the fire; not even a single fresh leaf and grass can be seen."

"Just check; find a safe place to deliver the package, and after that, we leave," Franky ordered.

Franky also tried to send a radio to the UW station on the planet but there was no reply; the station looked destroyed from afar.

Monica was the captain of the pilot group. Five Spacejets were sent down to the surface while five others guarded the ship with Monica. Five scouts were sent down into the storm clouds because there was indeed bad weather over the city of New Paris. An art that was covered in dark clouds of lighting and chaos. A dead beauty, the Grandeville, the great city, that seems abandoned, like a perfect painting hanging in an empty lone house with no one to see it. Planet Apen—the beautiful fallen flower.

A surveillance pilot said "Ah, captain . . . We received many shots from the ground! Many Anti-Air sharp homing bullets flew towards us like fire arrows. We will retreat."

"Finally, report was received," said Monica "Everyone leaves immediately, you might have entered the STARS-controlled zone, and they must have invaded the city."

But the fifth radio reconnaissance suddenly disappeared. Franky started to get worried and he said, "Oh crap, no one dies. I don't like paying insurance."

Hendrik looked at Franky and said, "Hey, boss, forget about insurance. If everyone dies, then you die, too."

Marco, the ship's Engineer, was standing in his room; he folded his arms, hoping that nothing would happen to his team, especially Monica.

Franky's ship advanced a little closer when it entered the atmosphere, a different airplane bearing the military code of Grande Military, a UW member. Those jets approached without saying anything.

Hendrik said, "Boss, there is a friend's plane, I tried to contact but no reply, and they should have contacted us first, right? Do they want to protect us?"

The Grande jet instead shot a rocket towards the ship. Spontaneously, five Franky Spacejets protecting the ship, fired back until the Grande jet crashed.

"Boss, we need to retreat a little further into space," said Hendrik. "It's a special type of classic air jet, they can't catch us in space."

Before pulling the ship, two Franky spacejet spies reappeared. One of the pilots said "Hey captain, boss! Anyone! Help us; three other spacejets have been destroyed by AA guns and have disappeared in the storms."

Like an eagle hunting bird in the sky, about twenty Grande air jets were chasing them from behind.

"Are they not the military of the planet? Apen colonies are part of UW — we are also part of UW. Why are they attacking us?" Franky asked, feeling worried and confused.

Hendrik replied, "Boss, maybe Star Ranger has mastered the planet."

"It's impossible," said Franky. "Star Ranger has never used an outdated plane; this is purely clear from the UW military."

Unable to dodge, the two Franky jets were shot down because they were already severely damaged. Twenty aircraft of Grande then chased the ship. Monica attacked them, and several drone planes were released to help. They chased each other until finally, Monica brought her spacejet down through the cloud.

Monica said on the radio as she suddenly saw the ruins of Grandeville, "Hey, boss. The whole city has been destroyed, everything has been burned from the forest to the ground. Everything is black and charred. We have to go back home."

Feeling upset, Franky then went into a spacejet that was quite large. Ten other mercenaries were there. While carrying the package, he said, "Monica, you and the others protect me; this package must be delivered so we can leave this damn planet. We can do this—don't worry."

Marco saw that and said to Hendrik, "Give me a plane, too, I will help them. Where are those bastards, the Central Army?"

"I don't know; they turned off the radio," answered Hendrik. "You must be careful, too; we need all the hands we can. I'll stay with this ship while observing the situation."

Then Marco climbed onto one of the Spacejets, but there was a pilot, so he hitched while helping from the back seat.

The pilot said, "Hey, you're the guy who teased my girlfriend Erica a few days ago, right?"

Marco was just silent. The pilot said, "Hahaha, calm down, friend. Hey, good luck next time to get a new girlfriend." Then both of them smiled.

Three more Spacejets came out, one of which had Franky. Marco followed to protect him from behind.

Monica saw that Marco had flown to the field and said, "Hey, Marco, what are you doing? Back on the ship! What if you get shot?"

Marco ignored her and said, "Take it easy, Monica. I will try to help."

They watched Grande's approaching military jets, many looking old and damaged. Of the twenty, a few were shot quickly, and many others even fell without being shot—like they ran out of fuel. More airplanes appeared, all of them bearing the Grande military logo which was part of UW.

"There are planes in this direction," Marco said.

When they turned their Spacejet towards the attacking Grande airplanes, the plane instead crashed itself onto a mountain while the propellers were still spinning. The gloomy weather was covered in clouds, but sunlight was still visible in the Apen star system; even a day looks like midnight. Everyone was confused. There were human pilots on the Grande Military aircraft, but they did not speak. They still push themselves to carry out orders while the old planes were running out of fuel.

Marco and the spacejet pilot flew after another Grande airplane, which they shot and succeeded in destroying the right wing of the Grande airplane; although a pilot escaped the plane with a parachute, it was evident that he was already dead.

Marco looked at it and said, "Ah, it looks like our bullets hit the poor pilot's body."

Marco's pilot replied, "I didn't shoot him, Sir Marco; I only shot his right wing once."

Something terrible happened: the Chicken's ship suddenly shattered in the air for some reason.

The pilot shouted, "NO, ERICA!" He then left the spacejet and let Marco drive the plane. The pilot flew away, but he was shot by one of the Grande air jets and killed in the air.

Marco tried to contact Hendrik, who was the ship's operator. He said, "Hendrik? Hendrik! Damn." There were no replies or a single word.

Seen from behind the clouds, like a large flash of lightning which destroyed their big ship, Franky, Monica, and Marco was devastated — their morale plummeted. One by one the spacejets were hit by lightning from above and fell. The bolt also hit Monica and Franky's spacejet, ruining it.

Their ship called The Chicken began to fall quickly into the middle of the city with the rest of the crew. Marco saw Monica and Franky's spacejet fall not far from the ship and chased them. He watched from the window as their spacejets were shot one by one by lightning and destroyed. Strangely, the flashes did not kill the Grande airplane that was flying with them. The remaining Spacejet pilots began to gather, but their streaks were hit by a massive ray. Marco became very shocked; he seemed to be the last spacejet in the air. Marco was then nervous, his hands trembling at the wheel, the worst thing that ever happened to humans—the feeling of loss, seeing people around them become ashes.

Marco, as the remaining leader, desperately ordered on the radio, "Anyone who hears, spreads, and seeks each other's safety. Get out of your spacejet or land it immediately!"

After all their pilots were hit by lightning, Marco became the only pilot in the sky. He flew in and crashed into a tall building, the bolt came striking hard until it was broken through the concrete of the building, Marco became unconscious. The dangerous situation, an unexpected terror of death itself.

* * *

After a few hours, he was finally awakened by a loud siren in the city. Marco limped out from the floor of building number six. He saw the city totally burned, but there was no smoke or fire, trees were dead, no grass was seen, and the silent city of Grande brought cold wind to the hearts of those who saw it.

In the sky, there were many transport planes from the Grande military—like eagles in the distance—that flew out of the clouds; then suddenly, there were many anti-air rockets and bullets that shot at the Grande planes, just as there had been another war going on there.

Grande's airplanes carried many paratroopers and circled them around the fallen ship of The Chicken from Marco's group. Many parachutes were flying; thousands of Grande soldiers were deployed from the sky.

Marco thought, *Why did Grande attack us, and with whom did they fight? Still, if I survived, then the others would also still be alive. Those paratroopers would pursue my other friends. Damn it! I have to go there to help them, but my jetpack was damaged due to a short circuit from a flash attack; my spacejet is also destroyed, I have to walk.*

He walked down the long steps, electricity in the entire city gone, making it hard to see because the building was dark; dark alleys made it difficult for Marco to walk. His armor was heavy so he threw it away there. Finally, he walked out the front door, and saw the word "HOSPITAL" on the building board in strange and different French accents.

"No wonder the corridors in this building are very complicated," he said.

CHAPTER 3

Cool air was confirmed by his geometer; good gravity, heavy rain, darkness — the city is not inhabited and reeks of death. The wind is very cold but no snows, only rubbish from the ruins of the city, but all the buildings are like the structure of the city of Paris, sculpted high up into the sky, like silent statues. After walking for a few minutes, the AA weapon was fired into the sky towards the Grande airplane. Some soldiers were patrolling from far away; suddenly, there were several soldiers there near him, they wore big helmets, and thick armor covered all their skin. The human-shaped army wore a uniform with the STARS logo from the Star Ranger large Juggernaut unit. One of them turned to look at Marco.

Damn, He thought. *They are Star Rangers, the Cyborg bastards who attacked this colony; the Apen military colony must have thought we were Star Rangers."*

The STARS cyborg army who saw him approach took out guns to shoot. From even a short distance, with cloudy and rainy weather, they had difficulty in hitting him; after three shots, they chased him with swords and axes because they were out of bullets. But their heavy armor was designed for range battle and not melee fighting, so it was weighty. The slow movements and building ruins made many STARS soldiers fall. Marco ran fast, then entered another building; he suddenly saw other STARS with mossy and dirty clothes standing there holding long-barrel guns who wanted to catch him.

I'm dead, Marco thought.

"DON'T MOVE!" shouted the soldier in a half-robotic voice.

The soldier pointed his gun at Marco's head.

"HEY, I've given up!" Marco shouted at the STARS soldier.

The soldier kept aiming his rifle at his head, then shot, but it did not have a single bullet, and only a clicking sound could be heard.

Marco kicked the STARS soldier until he fell and then Marco ran away. He continued to run until he came to a lake in the city; there were many bones in the lake and along the road. He became confused and lost direction; a STARS motorbike appeared from behind and shown a bright light on his face. The driver then chased Marco, who ran and jumped into the street until he arrived on a river bridge and was trapped.

"Damn; why am I in the middle of the bridge?" he said frightened.

A STARS armored car appeared from the front and the STARS motorcycle from behind. Both stopped and tried to shoot Marco. Marco bowed because the fence beside the bridge was too high to jump over. But the two machine guns on the vehicle ran out of bullets; then they stuck the gas to hit Marco. Marco screamed hysterically, but the two vehicles stopped because they ran out of fuel. The riders and passengers came out with Fire Axes and forks in their hands.

Marco laughed in fear. "What is this? You really still want to fight even though running out of resources? Are you crazy and thirsty for blood?"

Marco then ran past them all — their clothes were too heavy to make the movement so it was easy for Marco to pass them. After running for hours, Marco was tired. He sat to rest and watched the STARS troops chase him with wood and iron. Their movements were so slow that Marco relaxed but remained afraid. Seeing also the Apen Airborne troops who kept plunging from the sky made Marco excited to meet them.

"Oh, those bastards, even though they shot us for misunderstanding, were friends, so they are my only hope. At least I can get away from STARS cyborg," Marco said.

On the road, more and more bones were found, from small children to uniformed soldiers. Feeling sad to see many humans die, Marco was still eager to run. It was getting dark, the night had arrived, the red moon began to appear from the sky, and the red light was seen filling the ground with red color like blood. The ground seemed warm, the cold winds always blowing to chill the skin, but the true cold feeling will always stay in the lonely heart. Confused with death around him, he tried to not become one of them, while the dead bore through the walls and dirt, but mostly by time itself.

Why is the night like noon? He wondered.

The daytime scenery that had been dark then became like a real afternoon at night with red, yellow, and orange lights everywhere. Sirens continued to ring everywhere, Grande's military planes keep fielding airborne troops and STARS still shot them with AA guns and rockets. Trying to walk quickly, Marco decided to steal a car, many of which were filled with bones.

He said for those corpses, "Sorry, ladies and gentlemen, but your car is now mine now."

He removed them and tried to turn on the machine as best he could; even though there was a key that still hung, it turned out that all the electrical components with the engine had been removed and there wasn't any oil inside.

Those damn cyborgs must have taken it all. Damn, too, it turns out it's a long distance I have to walk, he thought.

When his tiredness peaked at midnight, he began to walk limply. Almost half-dead, his enthusiasm was the only thing that forced his will to walk through the valley of death, with little hope; dead bones became only dust to his eyes for a moment.

Even though there was a bright light from the reflection of the red moon, the ruins of the city made many roads closed. Feeling troubled while looking at the smoke of their ship, Marco continued walking toward it. After he found a STARS barricade, suddenly some big Grande Mecha came out of the gates from the underground and started shooting at STARS troops who guarded the barricade.

"There it is," he said, "My human army, the Apen military from Grande; I have to be able to go to them."

He then ran towards them. Many STARS soldiers ran together to attack the Grande's Mecha, but they only had wood and iron, so they were destroyed by Mecha. When Marco approached Mecha, it even shot at him.

"HEY, I'm human! Not Cyborg nor Ranger! STOP IT!" Marco shouted.

Those Mecha were ignorant, like a jet airplane; they shot anyone other than the Grande military. Some STARS came out with rockets, and, with massive RPGs, shot Mecha to pieces. The Cyborg army then scavenged the remaining bullets and released the spare parts from Mecha. Marco saw a human operator in Mecha with full uniform and helmet, but the operator was silent. That place was dangerous, and he began walking far enough to leave the area; he approached the smoke of The Chicken's ship. The battle of war never stopped; it's what humans always do, destroy and build from ash. They made a statue by their own blood and destroyed it by their own conflict.

The place was filled with dead trees, like tall pillars planted on the ground in black soil-like coal sands, standing sequentially like tombstones at burial sites. A place that was once green, filled with pine trees—a planet that was made to be like the living earth has become dead earth. Seen from the sky, the Grande Airborne parachute troops plunged closer to his position, many of whom were shot by STARS AA guns before reaching the ground. Marco saw one of them escape, then chase that Grande paratrooper. With enthusiasm, he then climbed a ruined building that was quite tall; the soldier fell on the roof. For nearly an hour, Marco tried to go up, even almost falling down; after a great effort he finally got to the top.

"Damn it again," he said dejectedly. "The Grande military army was actually in the next building."

Marco then jumped up and climbed down from the roof, moving to the next building where he reached the roof of the soldier.

From afar he looked dead. "Too late; it seems like this one is also dead," Marco said.

As he approached the soldier hanging on an antenna pole on the roof, Marco could see the soldier not moving at all. His uniform embodied the military logo of the UW Grandeville Air Forces. Moving closer, Marco then wondered and took off the dusty helmet of the soldier because there was no blood along his body. He was shocked to find only a skull in the uniform — a soldier who had been dead a long time. He saw again some parachutes falling in the middle street, and all the other airborne paratroopers weren't moving at all — like they were already corpses.

"What? They are all just corpses? Then why bother to get parachuted into the battlefield; everyone in the parachute is just a skeleton. Or is this some kind of distraction tactic?" Marco said to himself.

A STARS helicopter saw him on the roof and chased him to shoot him with sharp bullets. Marco then jumped from a height but was not injured because he slowly dropped to the ground. There appeared another Grande Mecha who shot the helicopter down; after the fall, the STARS pilot came out with his clothes on fire, and something shocking happened again. The STARS pilot's helmet was released—visible from his face was half a robot and half-dead skull; from his hand were just bones controlled by an exoskeleton with AI. STARS' eyes were colored red lasers, just dead cyborg shells that were made by robots entirely. When Marco turned his face to see Mecha Apen, it was seen below that the operator was only a corpse that had become bone. Mecha was driven by an automatic self-defense system or AI like airplanes and others with no real operators.

This is just a war between AI, there are no humans or biological beings on this battlefield, he thought.

The two then attacked each other, Marco was not spared from the attack, so he had to avoid it. He didn't waste any more time, and then walked towards the smoke from his fallen ship. It was seen that the wave of Grande's military airstrikes had stopped.

* * *

When he arrived, he saw many STARS robotic soldiers scavenging around the place, walking on patrol while picking up the remains. Many robots used flashlights, so their position was clearly visible. Working by night and day, the robots seemed to represent their creator, to feed his ages until death came with a time of the end. Marco slowly progressed while hiding; many of STARS were seen wearing full army uniforms without ammunition. Marco saw exo-robotic bodies mixed with skulls. They were all dead, walking corpses with the help of AI and the exoskeleton robot. Marco advanced invisibly until he was close to the ship, but many STARS robotic bodies walked around the ship's frame, lots of smoke blocking the view so that Marco had difficulty.

There is no time to be thrown away, Marco thought. *I have to be able to get in search of survivors. Who knows, maybe they are still safe in the emergency tube ship.*

The ground was hot; black sand was seen in all places; the place was charred like that city. Marco walked here and there in the haze without getting anything but the heat, but his mind is the one that burned his feelings.

He thought, questioning himself, *Is that lightning also destroying the whole city? But where's the lightning, why is it so strong?*

Walking wondering without anyone answering, he was increasingly confused and sad. Feeling frustrated, he continued to wander in the crater where the ship had fallen. The oxygen tube diminished, and he could not survive in the smoke without oxygen. Inside the smoke he heard the sound of a powerful engine, and a large truck was seen emerging from the smoke. The lights were very bright, and the truck began to carry the remnants of black sand along with the place.

Why? He thought when he saw STARS trucks carrying black sand.

Then it appears that the sand is the metallic fuselage that has become ash — metal ash everywhere. Slowly the smoke began to disappear after a few hours due to the wind, and it was seen that a giant skeleton of the Chicken's ship only had its metal bones. Suddenly a whirlwind grew stronger, as if a storm were approaching; as the wind cleared the smoke, red moonlight shone like noon because the surroundings were so bright. Marco realized that he was standing in the middle of the ship's body which was only ash remains. There were no bodies — nothing but ash and the bones of the ship. The red moonlight illuminating the place made him visible to the STARS troops who were scavenging around. As a bullet shot past him, Marco was shocked. Feeling afraid, he started to move away, even though the sand was blocking his leg movements.

"Don't move, STAY IN PLACE!" shouted STARS in a robotic

voice while chasing and shooting at Marco.

"Are they stupid?" Marco said while piqued. "They ordered me not to move but continued shooting."

A STARS soldier then took out an assembled arrow weapon that had been tied with a rope. They began to shoot at Marco who was running away; the sand of metal ash blocked his movement so that one of the arrows hit his right shoulder. The small arrow penetrated him but not too deep in his body; the tip of the bolt had a piercing hook that stuck on his pilot armor. The shooter pulled the rope back and took Marco towards him. With dead eyes and sickly machines, the STARS are like murder with one reason to live . . . to take another life.

Feeling sick, Marco tried to remove the hook from the arrow, but no avail; he had to take off his remain armor. He had no choice—he had to take off his clothes so he could run again; however, the rope was made of metal, and the shooter activated electricity on the string and made Marco fall helplessly. Seeing Marco fall, the shooter and other STARS came forward.

"Don't move, stay in place, we will come," said the STARS soldiers repeatedly. "We will come, don't move."

Feeling weak, Marco saw them approaching, then a miracle happened . . . a Grande airplane bombed them, and the STARS troops who were there ran around in all directions in a panic. A bomb fell on a STARS soldier, the explosion destroying his body as his bones flew left and right near Marco. The metal gray of the wrecked ship flew everywhere. STARS soldiers tried to shoot the aircraft, but they lacked effective weapons. Marco took the opportunity to pull out the hook and then stood up, left his remain armor, and ran again. Many of the bodies of the dead airborne troops were parachuting back. After being stopped for a few minutes, Grande's lifeless military airwave returned. Grande airplanes began to release more corpses of airborne soldiers with parachutes.

This time Marco advanced to get one and took the gun. *This weapon seems still to function even though it looks dry;* it was a type of Assault rifle named Clarion XL. *I'll try this,* he thought.

Pulling the corpse to a close hole to hide, he removed the uniform of the armor from the airborne body and put it on. With a vest and bullets, Marco began to feel a little confident.

He opened a food box and saw the expiration date: 2955. He was shocked. He thought, *Today is 3050 E.T., meaning this war happened a hundred years ago or fifty years according to the Apen planetary calendar.* Fearing that there might be nothing to eat, Marco began to move to find a safe place not far from where the Chicken ship had fallen.

There was a hotel not far away because the Chicken ship fell in the middle of the city. The hotel was still standing, but was in the state it had been burned a hundred years ago. He made his way up the high stairs, where he tried to monitor the area. From above the balcony on the eighth floor, he saw a vast landscape — the city and the sky was so lightless that danger and horror were awaiting in every corner. Marco looked out for the ship ash. He realized that when his craft fell, thick smoke visible from the sky was smoke mixed with metal sand. He rested there for the next few hours.

He continued to observe from the balcony of the hotel, but there was no movement other than the two corpse faction AI that were still fighting, STARS and Grande. The oxygen tube was almost gone, the clothes were hollow, and he had a shoulder wound. He was worried about being contaminated by bad air, poison, or radiation if it existed.

"I will die," he said as he became hungry. "There is nothing I understand about the planet. Something I know is that this place is dangerous so anything might happen. Unfortunately, none of the items from the ship survived." He then remembered Franky's spacejet and said to himself, "Maybe there are still a few things left because Franky's plane is quite large. There is a package there. And the package recipient? I will hit her face if necessary, and she makes us suffer."

Feeling annoyed, Marco also thought that he had to deliver the package that was the only goal that still existed besides surviving. After sitting safely for two hours, he began to feel hungrier; he wanted to go to Franky's plane but did not know where it was. A red flare came out of one of the corners of the city. Observing around him from high, he only saw a dead scene, from lifeless crafted buildings to inanimate machines that walked and flew with black souls, and created chaos.

Flare? Is that from Franky? He thought.

Then he went down to street level again, worrying. He said, "I don't know anymore; are there still people living here? I have no choice but to keep moving until the end when I can no longer move."

He went toward the light of the flare, but then the light disappeared. After memorizing the position of the flash, Marco headed for the shops around the quiet city. He saw many broken crates and houses, while the former owner was just a corpse, sitting on a chair, leaving stuff owned by no one. Passing the road of the dead man, the living man must hold his fear, or he becomes vain like the other.

CHAPTER 4

Hungry, he checked every corner only to find expired foods which were nasty with blackened colors. No choice, Marco put the food cans inside the bag that he found, in case there was nothing to eat later. He opened the drinks room at the store looking for mineral water, but it was difficult because almost all the bottles of colored drinks had lost their color. Then he opened one while smelling the water. He abandoned the most foul-smelling bottle, because there were still many bottles in the corner. After finishing looking for food and water, he went to various shops in the center of the dead city, looking for warm clothes, other meals, drinks, backpacks, and medical supplies. He found one by one. The oxygen tube ran out, but the battery for the AC was still functioning, so he tried to open the helmet to check the Apen air for the first time because he had no choice.

"Before it opened, I just wanted to say, Ariana . . . curse you and your Central bastard. Oh, my poor friends, forgive me if I die." Then he opened his helmet, and the air was inhaled. He still felt excellent—the wind did smell a bit burnt but okay, even for night air.

Not bad; whatever radiation and poisons do exist — but I hope not — the smell of this place is not much different from outer space, like charred.

The atmosphere was quiet again; there were no more waves of the Grande airplanes coming.

Maybe they are tired, he thought while looking at the sky.

Becoming more thirsty, he kept walking while drinking a little of the bottle he opened.

Marco said to himself while wondering and kept complaining. "The taste of these bottles is very bad, bad in the sense of not having a bitter taste but just bad. I don't know how to explain it. I'm confused where I'm going, but if the flares are nothing or just the robotic corpses of STARS soldiers on patrol, I'll go back to the city center, and there are lots of drinks and foods there."

After spending almost an hour there. Marco monitored the movement from the front. Apparently, there was a convoy of Grande military forces. Armored cars began to emerge from the road, one of the significant texts said: "Chien de Chasse" on the side of the vehicle. But it was also seen that the driver of the convoy vehicle was just a dead body; the vehicle was controlled by AI from a distant place. They represent the cycle that never severs, astir in their task, made by the previous people who died a long time ago, updated but nothing really new.

Oh, again. A convoy of a walking corpse, he thought.

Then a STARS soldier appeared from the front shooting a flare from his flaregun.

"So the flare came from him," Marco said, then he walked away and left the place.

Many STARS appeared to shoot the convoy; armored vehicles were equipped with AI defense systems, so they also returned unmanned fire.

Desperate, Marco headed for the Grande convoy in a Grande soldier uniform, hoping they would not shoot him.

Hopefully they think I am part of the army, and take me to their leadership, he thought as he walked down.

He then gets to a Grande car that runs unmanned. The vehicle's laser gun points at his head, and the vehicle stops.

Marco shouted, "WAIT, BROTHER! I'm human! I came with

a package for Mrs. Alexa," he said, even though he didn't have the package with him.

Then there was a pounding sound from the car's weapon. Marco realized that the car was trying to shoot him, but there were no bullets in the magazine.

"SCREW YOU!" He shouted again, then left, running away in anger.

He got some STARS appearing with stolen weapons they carried from dead bodies of Grande paratroopers. Those STARS immediately shot at him. He tried to take cover while firing back, but their numbers were increasing. Marco took shelter in a house, but then STARS started pelting it with grenades. The explosion made him hurt but was not fatal...

Blood came out of his head and the helmet was broken. Then he put the helmet inside his bag. *Who knows it can be repaired*, he thought.

He tried to walk, but he felt dizzy because of the explosion. He also felt stressed and frustrated — so much so that his health was in poor condition. He managed to escape again from them through the cracks of the city building. After walking a short distance, he found dark metal sand on the road. He touched the still-hot sand. While standing to monitor, he saw a Spacejet frame. He approached, but everything else had turned to ashes. Seeing too much death of the poor souls, their ghosts seem to haunt his feelings, with sounds of the dark terrifying his mind for no reason. The most painful feeling for a human is an eternal discord by death, forcing the memory to accept pain to dream.

Marco sat there and cried out in frustration. "Who is this? Where will all the survivors be? Come on, think, Marco! Think harder!" He was also afraid that it was Monica but kept trying to think positively while attempting to find Franky's Spacejet. He hoped its condition was not as bad as Franky's.

The city was extensive. So it was easy to hide in the vast area, but it was hard to find something.

In his heart, Marco continued to say, *Come on, Marco, think harder! What should you do? You can't just give up!!* He continued to question himself while beating his head softly in frustration.

After a long cry, his tears became dry; touching his head, folding his body, time makes him tired with sadness. He decided to keep looking; as he continued walking, he marked every road by spraying paint on the wall while writing anything to indicate that he had been there. He wrote "Marco Polo, Marco once here, the letter M, Hello, please, SOS" and so on. He continued to carry many bottles of paint, which he got from a shop. Then he made a plan to build a house post at the hotel near the falling ship the Chicken. He began writing the address of the hotel in every corner of the city he left. Marco also started to eat the stale food he got while closing his nose and swallowing immediately.

Marco spent most of his time feeling sorry for himself, waiting in the dead garden on a chair. He only saw a pile of bones everywhere. After almost a week, he continued to experience diarrhea. He had bandages all over his body because he kept running from the pursuit of the stupid AI-controlled dead soldiers for weeks. Walking with no direction, with the only mind to survive, he began to become bored. He looked at the sky, to the cloud, remembering his home planet, his friends, and his life. In a lone, dark time, a man will dream of his future that almost hardly comes true, or remembering his past, forces his view of himself to change, becoming sorry for himself.

Our ship the Chicken crashed and invited the airborne fleet to come out. As if someone had arranged them, I had to find out the origins of the Grande troops, he thought. Marco then began to get sick and sad, and he decided to find the headquarters of Grande as soon as possible.

Who knows? There might be humans there, he thought.

In bad condition, he decided to go further. He wrote on the

wall in the empty hotel where he was staying "Marco has gone far from here; if he does not return, he is dead or he successfully reached his destination."

He walked out of that place. This time it was farther and farther away from where he'd ever been. A broad highway was passed; then he saw black sand.

A spacejet plane again? He thought in wonder, and then Marco hurried to the place. The plane's frame was more prominent than the usual spacejet; when he digs the ground around, he finds a box.

He said loudly, "THIS DAMN BOX MAKES EVERYONE DIE BECAUSE OF IT!" When it was forced open, there was a smaller box inside.

Marco said, "Box again?" He tried to open it but couldn't, because the little box was locked dead and made with durable metal.

The box was quite light, so he carried it in his bag. He got the written address for Alexa postcode, which was located at Grande military headquarters at the end of the highway. The thing that brought them to the lust of money also died in vain handiwork of greed.

"It's time to work," he said irritably. "Sorry, boss, but I will retire after this."

* * *

He stood long enough to feel sad while looking at the sand; he knew that Franky his Boss had died there. There was nothing there besides the box that was wrapped tightly. Then he left to go to the Alexa location. The atmosphere was tranquil after that; there were no more gunshots from STARS, and no more bomb blast from Grande's military—they had stopped operating entirely.

"Surely AI has withdrawn their troops," he said, looking at

the lifeless city with no single human.

But there were still some STARS everywhere scavenging and making weapons, waiting for the next Grande military attack that somehow will happen. He walked for several days, making a temporary camp every night. But he never forgot during the day to look for those lousy food cans.

While pushing a wheelbarrow, he thought, *Look, Marco, you are now a scavenger just like the STARS robotic corpse, oh my . . .*

The place was quite open. Then he was shot at from a building far away. The shot missed. "Damn, Sniper weapon," he said as he ran pushing his cart.

He found a broken electric bicycle that he tied to his small wheeled cart, took it all while finding a shelter, and escaped from shooting range. One after another sniper shot missed until they finally disappeared. The shots came from STARS above the building. A massive motorway—Marco cycled all day long for fear of being shot again. Finally, the night with the red moon appeared. He didn't like the color, although it was brighter. Marco preferred day because it was dark and hard to see. Some storms make the weather darken during the day, but the weather was sunny when the night and moonlight make everything look bright like noon.

Oh, Marco, at least we came in a bad season; imagine if it were summer and there were no clouds. Surely your head would have been broken by shots for a long time, he thought, grateful.

After being far enough from his place of origin, he saw many STARS soldiers walking on the toll-road bridge that passed over the city, but they walked apart and alone. Marco shot them quietly with headshots. When he opened one of the STARS bodies he had killed and looked at his inventory, he got various items—lots of spare parts and oil.

They are like bees that collect honey, but for whom? Marco wondered while looking at it.

He then looked ahead at a large barricade with an aluminum

plank of wrecked cars made into walls. Many tires were scattered and thorn fences lined the place. In the center, there was a large door, guarded by STARS corpses and turrets. STARS also drive a giant Mecha robot stolen from the remnants of the Grande military. Marco's guts got sour, but he had to be able to enter.

"I came this far; I can't retreat," he said while whispering to himself.

It was seen that many STARS scavengers walked in rows to enter the gate. The gate was rusty, and the robots were dirty.

"Can't disguise myself; the robots must have sensors," Marco said. "Why, why am I asking myself this? Oh, dear."

He looked back, and there was a scavenger of STARS cyborg approaching; the robot looked broken and walked somewhat erratically. Marco snuck and managed to get behind the freight cart carried by the walking cyborg's corpse—filled with fear and hopes not to be arrested. The cyborg continued to pull the cart to the gate; the guard was quite stupid and let it pass by just checking the cyborg without checking his luggage. Behind the boxes and piles of rubbish, Marco lay in hiding. After he made it through the gate, he lifted his head slowly and saw a more massive barricade. This time the guard there checked the luggage. He jumped out slowly; apparently, he had reached the height of the toll bridge, so it was too high to jump. He saw not far away that the bridge was headed for a Grande military headquarters which had been controlled by STARS.

"What now?" he asked himself with a small voice. "There are at least eight layers of barricades as far as I can see."

Marco was trapped between two STARS barricades. The wind on the bridge was strong enough to bring sadness to his heart again. After a few minutes, he saw a Grande auto-pilot plane patrolling above that was controlled by AI. Marco wiped away his tears, put a damper on his weapon, and tried to shoot an airplane—hoping they would be affected and come out again to divert attention. Marco's shot didn't hit the plane, and finally, the aircraft left. He sat down, still waiting; after almost half an hour, another plane appeared and he tried to shoot it, but, again, there was no result.

Then he saw an AA gun under a bridge near the park. He threw a grenade at the AA gun right after the Grande patrol plane passed as if they were bombed. That was successful, and AA guns fired back at the aircraft until it was destroyed.

Good, what show do we have after this? Mine for sure, he thought as he sat waiting on the bridge fence.

Airplane formations appeared after almost an hour. Five planes were coming in the form of a V formation. The planes tried to bomb the bridge; STARS which were there panicked and shot back but the planes managed to dodge.

"What now, again?" Marco asked himself waiting.

The airplane was a bomber and started bombing the bridge; after everything was destroyed in the bombing, STARS troops began to scatter as expected by Marco. A line of other planes appeared. Marco ran towards one of the Mecha that was not in use while his guard was watching the air. It was known to others STARS nearby, so he had to shoot back while he retreated to the edge of the bridge and jumped.

The Mecha fell down a hundred and fifty meters, there was a gash that damaged Mecha's legs, so Marco had to run out with his feet. The Sniper and other STARS Soldiers were busy shooting the plane, so Marco managed to run to a dry water tunnel. He hid there while watching the outside. Because of the tight security around the bridge, he decided to inspect the dry water passage, which was under the toll bridge. To save the flashlight energy, Marco wore a torch that was burned by the oil he collected. Marco advanced slowly, fearing the darkness of the place.

"Wait, why did I enter?" He said as he was about to get out. Suddenly a gas explosion occurred because of his torch, and he fell. The place was burned by gas and exploded. There was a small fire in the place, He then saw a significant number of bones in the light of the fire.

Gas and people die? Whether this comes from their body or poisonous gas, he thought. Then he picked up a gas mask on the ground quickly and used it. "Good thing I found this, so I didn't breathe much gas."

The burning fire also burned the oil on the ground, and Marco saw that it was a hiding place. He found much anti-government graffiti there. It was like a hideout and refuge from a government attack. He walked and found lots of maps and photos. Marco was increasingly confused about what political conflicts were happening in the Grandeville. He saw many family photos and found the skull of a small child who was wearing a gas mask. That made his heart even more deeply saddened. Happiness, then a fight to live—that's how humans spent all their breaths in their lives; one step from the underworld of dead, they will no longer receive both pain and joy.

Everything died, from the air to the ground. What actually happened here? Some human skeletons were still inside their cars, some were still on the plane on their seats, and some corpses were still on the plane waiting to be parachuted. Did they all die instantly? Marco was increasingly shaken by the mystery, "WHAT HAPPENED HERE? SOMEONE SAY SOMETHING!" He shouted alone.

The silent bodies of the fallen, forgotten people from the past, poor souls that sleep forever in dust and worms. He saw only misery and the pathetic short lives of humans, where all of their vigor of mind rest forevermore in a vacuum with no words from their mouths, and the only story remaining is from a picture of their bones.

He then began to scavenge the remains of useful items while searching for information. Many papers like maps and notes told the history of the place. There was a diary book there written by a militia. "From Maximilien", Marco said as he read the diary, thanks to his little knowledge of French. "Our fight will never end; the government is only concerned about the elite. When world war broke out, everyone forgot our struggle about justice, but we will still fight. In the war there will be war. Many say that this world war was made by STARS to disrupt the security of the colony, but we also have enough evidence about government fraud against their own people. Pour la liberté."

After thinking for a while, Marco concluded: "Many old weapons; they are also fighters hiding from police chases. These are the most separatist protesters and rebels against their own government. But what is meant by world war? Is this country also at war with other countries? World war and inner conflict created by STARS, to make them weak and then the STARS invade entire colonies. Smart tactics."

The fire that burned the cloth and paper in that place began to disappear; many storage barrels of oil spilled but the fire continued to fade making the area increasingly darker. Marco turned on the flashlight he kept and began to take a walk for a while before finally deciding to find a way out of the underground. Then he saw another dry water passageway, its wall showing many bullets. From the front there were many bodies between the Grande police and Separatists. It looked like this was the fighters' last defense before everything somehow died. There was even a police officer who was still sitting in the car, while the others were sitting at the top holding turret guns and they all seemed to die instantly. Marco advanced to find several types of vehicles for this type of electric car. He tried to turn on the old vehicle and succeeded.

CHAPTER 5

"Let's go!" he said while raising the speed of the vehicle.

The vast waterway was quite extensive. As he rode along, he looked for a way out of the ground. Many large dead drones along the road became obstacles, so he had to turn around to look for another way.

When he got out of the ground, he found a wide-open road. Many bodies were scattered there; from the other side there were skulls of demonstrators, and on the other hand, many police corpses were strewn about while wearing full uniforms and shields. This part of the city was called New Paris and was very large; even many other cities were contiguous while dispersed throughout the country so that the nation was called Grandeville which means a big city.

Marco came out and checked. He said in his mind "All people died together; they were even like falling asleep in their respective rows. It was not possible for an explosion or poison gas to kill them—they seemed to fall like losing lives immediately without any movement." This made him very dizzy, and then asked, "But where is Alexa? Which faction does she join? The address is behind the high walls which are heavily guarded by the walking dead run by controlled robotic bodies from STARS AI brains."

A small security robot appeared—in a broken state and an unclear sound—the old robot runs on solar energy. Marco approached it because the robot seemed to have no weapons and was not aggressive.

"Hello, wheeled robot," he said, and asked "Can you help me?"

"Go away, soldier, the war is over," said the robot when he saw Marco wearing an airborne army uniform which he stole from the dead.

"Good, at least you are the sanest robot so far," Marco said praising.

The robot then walked away, leaving Marco. Like a person with no task nor master, the servant engine lost his will without the purpose of creation. After standing for a moment paying attention to the new place he was arriving at, Marco saw a bird flying above him. Feeling curious, Marco stepped forward to see the bird as it perched on the fence, obvious that the bird was dying with fleshless bones and, in its frame, was fitted with an exoskeleton and in his head was a robotic brain with red eyes. A terrible place to visit.

Man, I feel worried, he thought *The eyes of this bird are like Cyborg STARS that I often meet.*

Marco hurried back to the car and left there looking for another place. There was a small map in his hand that showed the location of Grande's military headquarters, so he went there, hoping not to get a high wall made by STARS.

A siren came from a police car following him.

The officer in the police car said, "Bonjour, Monsieur, please get out of the stolen car. The car belongs to the Grande police department—you have no right to use it."

Hearing a human voice, Marco became excited and stopped the car. The police car approached and stopped right beside him. It was seen that the police car was controlled by a small ball-shaped robot on the steering wheel and the human voice was only a speaker from AI.

Trying to behave normally, he said, "Sorry sir. I only borrowed it to get towards my military headquarters," while pretending to be a Grande soldier.

A large turret came out of the police car. Marco quickly drove away, the turret shot missing.

"Ah, damn! Crazy cop. Using a strange way to pull me over," he said irritably.

The police car then chased him, still shooting. Both police cars had thick layers of steel, making it difficult to penetrate. Marco tried to cheat the robot by turning suddenly and other tricks. But the robotic police was agile and kept right with him. Marco saw a STARS post farther away and headed for it, but the police car that ran after him stopped as if he didn't dare to advance.

It's not wrong anymore, he thought. *All the Grande robots are also controlled like STARS robots — both of them are bastards."*

Sniper bullets began hitting the car. Marco checked the control of his vehicle and got many weapons' buttons.

"Is this a police or military car? Oh, it must be a special anti-terror vehicle from the Special Police," he said after accidentally firing a rocket.

The rocket worked well and destroyed the STARS gate post in front. Marco then drove in; not long after that, many vehicles bearing the STARS logo appeared from behind. The STARS vehicles looked like steel cars assembled with knives and rifles. When his car was shot, a large military drone named Cerberus emerged from above and shot STARS cars. Some drones also chased and shot Marco's car. There was a button that said auto-shoot. Marco squeezed it, and a turret gun appeared in his car roof to shoot all the enemies. The chases took place between Grande drone, STARS, and Marco's car.

Marco saw that there was a gate that could pass through the wall that surrounded the military headquarters; he then entered crashing into another barrier after shooting it with a rocket.

"Yes, just like in a movie!" He yells.

More and more Grande police drones came chasing and

shooting around. After entering the military territory controlled by STARS, Marco saw large piles of metal trash everywhere — reminding him of recycling sites.

STARS automatic defense system issued various types of motorbike auto-pilot vehicles with wings that can fly in the sky. Then the air became chaotic because of the battle between the Grande Cerberus drones and STARS motorbikes. A large "SR"-shaped monument was carved in that place, and many military bases were used as trash collection sites.

Confused about the direction, Marco looked at the map and said, "Oh, look, this and that corner. Let's see if there's a way there. Wait, I don't even know the meaning of this map." He continued to drive his vehicle despite being shot at from various directions.

* * *

There was a massive tower in the middle of the place. Marco circled in search of the road to the tower but had difficulty because it was in the middle of the STARS area. A city siren controlled by STARS again rang, and a new wave of Grande military aircraft appeared for the third time. After many Grande drone police drones were destroyed, the military forces retook action.

"Oh, look at these fools. They detained airborne troops again. Didn't realize that they were all corpses! STARS will take advantage by stealing weapons from airborne corpses," he said to himself.

But this time the waves were different, not only did the airplanes field Airborne's human paratrooper corpses but also many of Grande's still functioning military police robots named Marsouin. Although military police robots are actually just supportive they are the only soldiers with motion. Many parachutes were shot before getting to the ground by STARS; then the airplane pulled out many tubes containing soldiers and armored vehicles controlled by automatic AI. Several containers arrived safely on the ground. When the tube door opened, only the Marsouin robot troops came out while the human army just sat like corpses in a container with full armor while wearing complete weapons and steel helms that covered their faces.

"Enemies are everywhere," he said. "It's really chaotic, but it's fun!" Laughing in fear, Marco advanced with his armored car toward the tower.

He hit anything on the road, which moved or did not move. A scavenger robot was caught by him, and the robot dropped plenty of things including oil which wet the windshield. Marco tried to clean it, but the glass cleaner had been damaged from the car because of a traffic jam. Marco turned the camera on, but the camera was too dusty. Unable to see, he used electronic maps from satellites, but that didn't work either because there were no satellites in the sky.

"I will protest to the mayor and the president; this city is very unfriendly and chaotic!" He said jokingly while angry.

Because he could not see, he slowed the speed of the vehicle, but then he was hit by a police car that chased him but had stopped outside the gate. The vehicle pushed him until both of them went into a garbage pit—both stuck and jammed. Marco shot the car with the remaining rockets until the weapon from its turret was destroyed. He got out of his car and backed away to get the car door, shot the robot through the window but the glass was bulletproof, and finally, Marco left there on foot while leaving the two police cars trapped in the hole. He walked to the big tower but didn't know where to go. He saw an electric machine close to that place.

Hmm, this is Grande's headquarters which is controlled by STARS. Who knows? If I activate electricity, then many Grande robots who fell asleep will get up from the quarters to shoot STARS, he thought.

He then advanced to the machine and entered the empty buildings around it looking for buttons or anything to light the place. He read and looked for the direction of the operator room. There were several automatic turrets along with the room which made it difficult for him; he shot several of them while moving forward. There came many secular robots without rifles that only wore electric batons that no longer functioned. Marco shot everything while advancing. His bullets were almost gone; he had to keep moving but was blocked.

Seeing a few parachutes descending outside, Marco came out again taking the bullets from the corpses. "Gracias, muchas gracias," he said jokingly to the dead, and then went back to the building.

* * *

After a few small battles between himself and security robots, Marco made it to the operator station. Unsure which button he needed, he got a lever on the power button and pushed it. There was no reaction in the building, so he walked out and saw that only the tallest tower in the middle of the base was lit.

A lamp in the small monitor in his clothes power up, "There is a sign here," he said. He turned on the monitor phone in his left hand. That stolen Grande soldier uniform contained many things.

There was a button that wrote the command center "Here it is, the person who controls the Grande military!" After fiddling with it, the screen resets and turns off.

What? Again? He thought desperately.

Trying to turn it back on, Marco decided to contact Grande's command center through the screen.

Suddenly connected, it said, "Please wait a moment."

The screen of a video call from an unknown woman finally

appeared.

"You must be Alexa!" Marco said excitedly.

"It's impossible," said the woman. "Are there still active soldiers after all this time, qui es-tu?"

Marco replied, "No, a dead soldier lent me this shirt. I am just a package deliverer. You ordered a package, right?"

"Oui, Monsieur Marco, as soon as possible, bring it to the command center located above the tower," said the woman.

Strangely, Marco said, "Miss, please pick me up and command your troops to stop shooting me."

"Sorry, I can't," she said "I have lost control; everything here has now become auto-pilot. The troops came from other provinces because they had their own command system. My army has long been destroyed. Look around this headquarters; no one is still alive—only crazy independent AI from the police headquarters and a crazy one from the next province with their paratroopers."

"I will get there," Marco said and then turned off the screen. In his heart, he wanted to scold the woman but kept it for later.

There were lots of garbage piles, taken from various regions in New Paris. Junkyard spread widely fond memories of decayed fragilities, a hoard of obliterated bodies, to think no more, like the rest of the planet. He walked and found many STARS factories made in assemblies. Those factories made many garbage robots, which are a type of robot assembled from various objects called Junker, are fragile, have three legs, and are equipped with multiple weapons from a small pistol to large saws. The Junker sprang at Marco, but he was able to dodge until he managed to get himself cornered in another building. Marco entered a barracks, and found many bodies of soldiers still asleep on their beds; the barracks were so long that he just kept running straight ahead through the doors, and Junkers chased him from behind with their handguns. The commotion invited the Grande robot to be deployed. A light-blue-colored supportive soldier named Marsouin pierced the roof of the barracks and jumped down. With Clarion's bullpup-type weapon, Marsouin quickly destroyed many STARS Junkers. Marco continued to walk forward while shooting everything that moved.

He called the video back for Alexa and said "Alexa! I continue to be trapped here and will die before I get there. Isn't there any help that can come?"

"Continue to move" Alexa replied. "Continue to run through many paths, and don't stop."

"Great help, merci . . . " Marco said irritably.

He arrived outside the room, where he met the police drone called Cerberus, shooting at him from behind. It shot at everything, including Marco, Grande eastern province robots, and STARS. From the left and right sides of the building, there were more and more Junkers coming in—even hundreds of them were approaching. All STARS Junkers were marked with a green cloth as a flag. Marco continued to run, jumping up and down from the roof until he finally fell into the other barracks building. The Grande armor he wore was very helpful in holding small bullets from the enemy, but it did not last long because several bullets penetrated and slightly injured him. The farther he ran, the more waves of Junkers; they even used arrows assembled with spears made from trash.

A Junker emerged from the front carrying a shield and ax. Marco shot his head then took his shield while saying "I am borrowing this!"

With that shield, Marco ran forward while holding the arrow from the Junker. Several Grande airplanes began to fall from the sky, running out of electricity fuel or being shot and made the situation even noisier. The barracks buildings continued to connect, so Marco continued to run past the windows and all the doors in front of him while heading towards the Tower.

Alexa called "I have activated the Tower defense that I control; all the turrets will help you shoot both STARS and Grande forces from the eastern province."

"Finally, something useful!" Marco answered.

Alexa's turrets shot many enemies from above, but several shots almost hit Marco, knocking him down.

"Watch your shot!" Marco said to Alexa.

A Junker appeared and almost sawed his neck, but Marco kicked him away then shot his leg because a Junker's head was protected by steel. The distance between the barracks and the tower was not so far, but Marco could not walk straight because the enemy was everywhere, so he had to run left and right.

"I've almost reached the Tower door, so watch your turret, lady," he said as he moved forward.

Alexa opened the door, and Marco entered the building and walked up a long staircase. The stairs were very high and he had to climb to the twentieth floor to reach the Alexa room on the top floor. While walking up, Marco became very tired, fell down and got hurt, and was overcome with diarrhea. Alexa's turrets managed to repel the approaching Junkers and Marsouins.

Marco sat on the tenth floor and said "Madam, I need to rest for a while."

Alexa saw him through the building's camera and said "Throw away all the items from your bag, I have many more-useful items above."

"I need food and medicines that don't expire," Marco said.

Alexa replied, "I have everything, in good condition."

Feeling impatient, Marco stood up after sitting for almost fifteen minutes and made his way up to the top.

"Open the door," Marco said. He wondered, *Why make this command center as high as this? What's wrong with making it in the soil? You are easy to shoot — weird.*

Alexa opened the door and Marco entered. Inside the lights, the room is in the fifth layer of the Tower on the top floor. The tower then slowly descends into the ground.

"Oh, so this tower can enter the ground," Marco said.

After all parts of the building had entered the underground, the gate closed from the top to make their tower hidden. A door opened again for Marco, and he entered but remained ready. He saw a woman standing among many computers; the bodies of the Tower operators were all over the seat in a state of stillness wearing headsets.

* * *

Marco stepped forward and wanted to give a hand greeting "Nice to meet you. Who are you, mistress?"

But Alexa did not want to give a handshake and just said "Welcome to the city of bones, bones of the living and the dead. I am one of the captains of the Troupes Coloniales or TC in the Grandeville Republic. Alexa."

Marco continued "Well, I want to say something. I hate you."

"Why, Monsieur?" asked Alexa.

Marco replied "I lost all my friends just because we delivered your damn package. This is not worth the lives of them or me. I want to go home! Take this package and show me the way out. Pay me with anything you have."

Alexa said, "I'm really sorry to hear that—I mean it. But please, put the package on the table there, and then the package will open automatically. Okay?"

Without asking again, Marco put the package box on a table and the package opened by itself. When the lid was removed, Marco saw that it was empty.

"Nothing, wait . . . Is this empty?! What is this, a joke!?" Marco said with a face full of emotion.

All of his struggle, worth nothing more than his own soul, he feels all of his sacrifice to money gone with no value. The man then looked at Alexa with a sharp look full of anger.

Alexa said something that surprised him "Listen, Monsieur, you are the package."

Feeling confused while rolling his eyes up, thinking of any logical reason, Marco said: "You got the wrong person."

Alexa said again "No, I'm not mistaken."

CHAPTER 6

"Okay," Marco said. "Are Ariana and the Central robots having something injected into my body or my friends secretly? Because whatever it is, take it, I'm sick of it! Take your money if necessary. I want to go home."

"No, Monsieur, we need only you; we need a human here, whoever he is," Alexa said.

Marco reacted. "Oh, so you need a man? I am not interested in giving birth here to fill the planet. This place is dead."

"That's not it, Monsieur," Alexa answered, then pointed to a monitor.

The screen began showing a video about the origin of the war on the planet.

Alexa spoke while the video on the screen described the atmosphere that had happened before. She said: "In 2900, the Apen colonies were pitted against others because a leader in the north was brainwashed by STARS in secret; it led to a world war between countries from the Northern Hemisphere and the Southern Hemisphere. The war led to weakening our government and destroying our economics. It was a STARS tactic — they invaded our planet against both sides later."

After hearing the statement, Marco asked "Fine, I understand. But why did everyone suddenly die?"

Alexa continued, "They died not because of the world war but a wave of dead."

Becoming increasingly curious, Marco stood and asked, "So?

Why is your robot still alive and what wave is that?"

Alexa answered. "The world of other planetary colonies is too slow to act; people from the south created a weapon called Nova that was taken from a distant galaxy, but something bad happened—the secret weapon exploded and killed all humans, cyborg STARS, and the whole planet. The wave of Nova raised an astral creature called Dragon because that's where the energy comes from, the wave of energy Nova exploded killed all the big biology. Only a small part of the robot survived and small creatures like bacteria. I called that a Nova Blast. On the highest mountain on the planet Apen, there is a military-sized castle as well. But that place is ten times more dangerous than this place. It is controlled by a dragon that lives and hides on the mountain, while its plasma army-like Phoenix keeps the atmosphere on the planet, killing everything which comes in or out. Look, this planet has never been active until now; your existence invites a lot of sleeping forces like from the Grande East province's self-defense system and STARS themselves."

"Straight to the point, lady; what do you want me to do?" Marco asked again.

"Help me," replied Alexa. "Beat the Dragon who killed the whole planet and your friends, to set us all free from Dragon's control of our atmosphere."

Marco said "You know, madam, my enemy is the person who killed my friends—actually Ariana because he sent us to this hell. After all, why don't you go by yourself?"

Alexa again replied, "Dragon wants to destroy all biological beings that exists. If you are here, then you will trigger it out. He was surrounded by many plasma creatures that were energy astral beings that did not let anything out or enter. Even large UW fleets who entered were easily defeated—five hundred million elite troops were killed in space. It stops them from entering this planet, but you somehow survived. UW is even afraid that if they destroy the planet, Phoenix and Dragon will fly out to another planet. So they sold this dead planet to Central for experiments. They probably send you as part of learning about Dragon's power."

"I'M NOT INTERESTED," Marco shouted firmly. "Just pay mercenaries or send your robots; why should I suffer?"

While looking like he was breathing, Alexa said, "They have done all that; for a hundred years, there have been thousands of times Central sent humans and androids. Only two people have succeeded so far. The first happened ten years ago, He was named Lee. He lost all of his fleets entering through the atmosphere guarded by Phoenix, and then he gathered a great deal of information and planned to get out. All troops in New Paris helped him. It made Phoenix attack us and destroy this base including Lee; he was killed ten years later, and this place was already overrun by STARS when you appeared. You're a miracle."

Marco became very scared and angrily said, "That's ridiculous! If millions of people died, how can I be able to do it alone? You said all humans died a hundred years ago; how could there be humans like you who are still alive in here?"

Marco threw an empty package box toward Alexa, but the box floated through Alexa's body, and he realized that Alexa was just a Hologram.

Marco reacted. "Oh, you're just a hologram! Of course, you are only AI. It makes sense now."

"It's true," said Alexa with a sad face "But I was actually killed a hundred years ago. Now it is only the memory of the brain lifted from my original body a day just before Dragon's Nova blast ended the lives of all the major biological organisms on the planet. Whether I am an AI or human is questionable. The type of AI I am was named as a Replica or Replican, and all the original body Replicas were killed when the memory of their brains was lifted first. I am a Replica type with a Hologram, most Replicas have body and face shapes resembling their original shape a hundred years ago, all thanks to the Android body technology from Central."

"Sorry to hear that. Are there other people deployed right now?" Marco asked.

"Those poor people will not reach the ground; the number of Phoenix attacking is by the strength of the opponent, and they're mighty. In the sky where they get sunlight or stars, they know every foreign object that enters or exits the planet atmosphere and destroys it. You are a miracle here, I don't even believe it. They sent many people from various colonies in secret. Look, out of hundreds of trillion humans in the galaxy, no one will care about you anymore; you're a dead man if you don't want to help me. But so far there has never been a military Grande that has risen. It seems that someone has activated them—this airborne attack is not unusual," Alexa answered.

"So, I'm just an experiment," Marco said irritably. "They are testing the best person who can go to the mountain. Still, this is stupid. I have no choice, even this is what those Central bastards hope."

After seeing Marco's somewhat obedient behavior, Alexa said, "All this is your choice; you may refuse, and you may join. If you join, then I have a request that you have to do. If not, then I'm sorry, but defeat the Dragon is the only way out of this lonely planet."

"Say it," Marco asked.

Alexa answered, "Go to Rivière province in the south of New Paris. It's a city on a big river, but more like a wide lake. STARS doesn't attack the area because it's difficult; go there and collect the remaining robot alliance from Garde de Grande—they are the ones left from our military which are still under our control. STARS Robot automatically, without a leader, still launches an attack even though there is nothing left on the planet."

Then Alexa found the area that had a jet named Chasseur, which Marco could use.

Marco asked, "Madam, tell me why, during the day the atmosphere gets dark, but the curfew is bright like noon? Is the reflected light from the moon stronger than the sun itself?"

Alexa replied, "As you can see, our atmosphere is controlled by the Dragon army called Phoenix. Phoenix keeps the planet all day long, so they take energy from sunlight if it is daytime and make the weather like a dark storm in the clouds. But if it is night, they stop taking light and make clouds less so that the red moonlight shines on this place like it was in the daytime."

Marco said to Alexa "That is extremely horror. Look, I will rest and sleep for a while. What about our crew? Did anyone possibly survive?"

Alexa said, "I don't know, but I will deploy my remaining robots from the Tower to look for them. Electricity has just been lit, merci mille fois! This place has been dead for ten years since the last survivor who arrived at this Tower was killed by Dragon."

Marco decided to rest for one day, preparing himself to go to the province in the south. Strangely enough, food was readily available; many plants were grown from stored dead seeds. It was like all that has been prepared for him. Finally, the things he wants the most on this planet appear, a will to make himself at home, with a soft sofa bed and better food. Sitting there, he forgot all of the pain from his wounds, then he slept like never before.

* * *

"Give me the best equipment and weapons!" Marco said a day later.

All the best from the tower was given, and Marco was ready

to board a plane that was still in good condition at the Tower. Marco then boarded the jet.

From behind, Alexa said, "Bonjour Monsieur Marco, avoid the east because there are enormous Grande defense systems that wildly shoot anyone; avoid big cities because there are Gendarmerie police who are still actively attacking foreigners and don't go too far south because there are troops of robots from southern countries who may be active. They are all controlled by an AI defense system that automatically functions without humans."

"What about STARS?" Marco asked.

"It's a pity," Alexa answered "You can't avoid them, STARS for a hundred years have continued to develop in their destruction just like the Grande military but are more savage. Remember, I will activate several satellites in the sky to communicate with you, so don't hesitate to ask me."

"OK, still contact me. Remember, too, I did this because I had no other choice," he said, closing the jet door.

The situation outside was getting calmer; there were no more Airborne attacks from the eastern provinces that provoked STARS troops. It was as if they were all just out waiting for Marco's arrival. The engine was turned on, all systems looked good, and, with a background as a Mercenary, Marco was used to it all. The jet was quite innovative even though it was made a hundred years ago. He quickly came out not too high in the sky but still lowered the plane because if it flew out into space a little, then it would invite a Phoenix attack. After flying for almost half an hour, Marco considered the surroundings from the sky—storms were everywhere, there were no trees, and all the land and buildings were black like they had been burned.

"The Republic of Grandeville," he said fascinated. "As the name implies, it really is a big city. The city looks like it is connected uninterruptedly—truly a dense planet. Unfortunate poor souls—without any warning, they all died instantly because of Dragon wave."

The same feeling appeared when he reached the planet for the first time, but now it's different, he's alone. Still shocked with his surrounding, only scorched landscape cross the eyes, with storms above, he feels like he's in the middle of two volcanoes, one on each side and upside down.

Alexa then called Marco. "Monsieur, listen. Stay on path, look for a large Eiffel tower in the southern province and land the plane there. Don't fly too south—you can trigger the sleeping system of the southern defense AI."

"Alright," Marco answered.

But in his heart he did not believe, so he wanted to test Alexa's words. Marco quickly directed his plane through Rivière province and into the border region of the country in the south. He lowered his plane slightly closer to the ground and saw no difference between the Grande Country and the South.

"This aircraft is quite fast," he said.

Alexa knew what Marco was doing and said "Monsieur, I know you don't believe me. But I remind you; if you even use the plane to get out of space then you will cause your death."

"I just looked around," he replied. "I am curious about this planet. Let me go around the world a little."

Suddenly a warning appeared from the radar; many missiles had been shot from the ground. His jet plane was quite advanced so he could avoid them, and Marco instead shot down all the weapons below.

"Oh, look—lots of dead tanks and corpses on the ground." He then flew his plane to shoot and destroy many of the targets below.

Marco struck the buildings, cars, trains, and everything that caught his eye in the southern hemisphere countries. Then he saw the south military headquarters and also shot it. After using hundreds of bombs and hundreds of thousands of bullets, Marco returned to the Tower where Alexa was. Everything looked like a toy from above, a miniature of real life, with no soul in the horizon; He could do whatever he wanted.

After entering the gate and landing the plane in the Tower, he got off the plane and said "Wow, this was amazing. Really relieved my stress."

Alexa appeared and was angry. "Monsieur Marco, what are you doing?"

"Look at the good side," he said. "I taught myself, and at least, I destroyed your old enemies."

Getting angry with Alexa, he said, "Everyone is dead. Respect them. Everyone I know is dead. Even I know that I am just a walking dead, too! There are no enemies here, only political issues made by STARS—all humans are brothers."

Marco continued, "Forgive me, Alexa, but I am no different from you. I am just like a walking corpse, waiting for the time to die for real. This is all because of Ariana. I will kill her and Dragon. Yes, I will destroy them all."

"You are the only soldier left," Alexa said. "Be a hero; then all the wealth on this planet will be yours! I don't care about everything. I just want to take revenge for all those who have the right to live but died in vain on this planet. Destroy STARS and Dragon. We almost made peace, but they foiled everything."

"Okay," he said. "I'm not your soldier, but fine. I will take revenge for all who died here. I will destroy Phoenix and Dragon. I promise. If my promise is not kept, it means sorry, I am dead."

Marco then loaded all the bullets and bombs on his plane. He prepared to fly again to the sky, this time to Rivière. After everything was ready, Marco directed his plane and headed to the place he was supposed to go from the start. Straight to the south, he saw many things that seemed like a silent mountain of buildings, but in manmade structures that were empty, the same with quiet inhabitants. They're all silent in misery, but in the sorrow that no one can see. After a short, long-distance trip due to the speed of his Chasseur plane, Marco arrived in the city of Rivière.

"Monsieur," Alexa said on the radio. "Land the plane on the main Eiffel tower. It is larger than the other Eiffel."

The city of Rivière was in the middle of a big river, so the place looked like the sea. It could be seen that there were many towers such as Eiffel; all were huge and had many buildings inside. There were also many ports and ships under the towers, but the place even looked dead and dark — just like the capital of the Grandeville in New Paris where Alexa lived.

After looking at the situation — the place was entirely silent — Marco landed his plane on the most massive Eiffel tower there. "Good, lady, I have entered the airport in this tower," he said.

Marco's plane entered an airport in the center of the tower behind the tower's iron frame. Before long on the dark runway, Marco heard a military-style dance trumpet sound, coming from the air control building and blasting through all the speakers in the place. A big river like the ocean, with horizontal blue dye waters and indigo towers, spread across the windy weather.

"Alexa," Marco asked via phone video, "What happened here, is this some kind of welcome? Apparently, there is still a little electricity here."

Alexa replied, "Welcome to Dunkirk tower — the largest Eiffel tower. Continue on foot, and meet Colonel Gustave and the servant robots that he assembled into soldiers. They are waiting for you."

Marco descended from the plane and walked without a flashlight because there was a little light coming into the tower iron frame that was wide open. Many specks of salt dust, blow hot and cold winds, fickle between rows of columns, the sounds of iron singing like a cry. He saw depth inside while strolling in the lost paradise.

The Colonel must be just a robot, he thought.

He had guessed right. Marco saw a fake mustache, a large-headed humanoid robot, dressed in a green Colonel uniform, wearing a great and canned steel helm. The big-head robot was also followed by a large group of other giant-head robots who wielded large steel helms; their helms were cranium with a star logo.

The robot said, "Welcome sir. My Army Men have been waiting for you."

"You must be Colonel Gustave. Sorry to make you wait a long time," Marco said.

The Colonel replied, "No problème, sir. I live to service my country, or what's left from it. I stand here for one hundred years. Don't be afraid — I and other Marsouins are your friends. Follow me."

Gustave's Marsouins do not even look like Marsouin; they're civilian robots modified to become soldiers. Marco was taken by elevator to a restaurant on the tenth floor. After arriving at the restaurant, he was invited to sit at an elegant white table.

There was a red flower there, and Marco became curious. "Wow, the only flower so far," he said, but when he touched the flower, it turned out it was a plastic flower. "Ow, of course," he said, laughing.

After sitting for a while, many other robots came out of the restaurant; the servant robots came with wheeled legs and served a meal. Marco sat quietly watching, knowing what he expected to happen. All the food was blackened, and the fish had become bone. No matter how beautiful, how wonderful, everything is slowly decaying, even now already destroyed.

"Thank you, Colonel, but I am full," he said, rejecting all the terrible dishes.

The colonel sat next to him and said "Sir, I have prepared

troops for you; you can attack the mountain where the Dragon is at any time."

His enthusiasm dropped, Marco tried to stay healthy and think positively. "We will win," he said.

"Excuse me, sir, please wait a moment," the Colonel said and walked away leaving Marco alone.

While he waited, Marco used his radio to contact Alexa. He asked, "Madam, why are the robots here friendly?"

Alexa replied, "They are part of our network that is still in control, they remain independent but not like AI from other provinces that have gone wild."

"Good," Marco said, "At least some robots are still sane."

Alexa continued, "Right, Monsieur. The Gendarmerie and Garde de la Grande have gone wild. They should be our helpers, but being out of control for a hundred years makes them take many stupid and irrational decisions. This planet are still very egoist even for an AI."

CHAPTER 7

A group of small, crafted Marsouin robots appeared, with uniforms painted poorly in green. They came to respect Marco's presence.

"Why me? I am not part of the Apen planet and not even a soldier," Marco said.

One of the robots said, "Monsieur, you are the only human, our creator, and we have no purpose without you."

Alexa heard that, too and said, "Listen, Marco, as the only human here you must be able to avenge us."

From the outside, there are many Grande military planes used by Gustave robots. From uniforms and logos to the fuselage, everything was painted green in contrast to the original color that was blue. The number of infantry there were thousands; hundreds of small, assembled propellers and several giant military balloons called Zeppelin were also present — actually taken from the tourism sector. A place that used to be the best journey of fortune now has become a journey of the fight, like every war that happened in the past.

Seeing that, Marco was shocked. He told Alexa, "This is a scene that I have never seen before, just like the story of the world war era on earth a thousand years ago."

Suddenly a robot near Marco was shot by a plane from the outside; their restaurant was indeed on the edge of the tower, so it was visible from the outside. The aircraft was the STARS plane that was sent to ambush Marco.

"Alexa!" Marco said.

"Yes, Monsieur?" Alexa answered.

Marco asked in a panic, "How come STARS can chase me here? What's wrong with them?" Then he began running into the room.

Alexa replied, "Don't panic. From the very beginning, they invaded the planet, intending to master it. They are Cyborg factions which are a mixture of corpses and bone machines. Maybe AI STARS sees you as their threat to rule the planet, even though their original army were killed by dragons a hundred years ago."

"I am sure there is no Star Ranger who wants this dead planet," Marco said. "If they want to continue the invasion from space, then many fleets will come. It's has been a century with no invasion, Star Ranger must have left their robots to roam like crazy here."

Many STARS planes were old-model Spacejet types that have a better quality of fighting than Gustave's aircraft. So Gustave had trouble protecting Marco.

"Monsieur" Alexa ordered, "Please get back into your plane; that's the only hope you can survive."

Marco ran to the airport while watching the tower being shot by many STARS spacejets. Some STARS soldiers were deployed with ropes from the spacejet, exchanging fire with the Gustave Marsouin robot that was there. Other soldiers from both sides did not have machine guns or bullets, forcing them to go forward with axes, saws, arrows, ropes, wood, and swords. In desperation, the struggle of the warriors will continue to be carried out in their distress; in limited choices, they must use all kinds of benefits from the limited opportunities no matter how sore it is.

"Stay behind me; I'll cover you, MONSIEUR!" shouted a Marsouin robot.

While wearing the shield they stole from the bodies of the

Gendarmerie and using Clarion weapons they took from Airborne's corpse, STARS began to easily advance. The restaurant was quite large, so STARS entered and trapped the smaller Marsouin robot groups.

Because of the situation, Colonel Gustave ordered his troops: "Lieutenant, start the explosion of this place!"

"Ready, Monsieur," said a robot, then left to trigger explosives near it.

"WHAT?!" Marco shouted in fear and confusion.

"I thought you guys were sane?" Marco asked.

Colonel Gustave replied, "Sorry sir, but I never said that."

The place then exploded, and the entire floor around them collapsed and fell on the floor below. It continued so slowly to decline until they were blocked and entered the bottom level. Many troops of STARS and Gustave, who were trapped, were also destroyed. Amazingly, Marco survived thanks to the incredible pilot armor that he wore. Colonel Gustave was still alive and functioning well. He got up, and Marco stood and took him to the bottom floor with a port.

* * *

After arriving at the bottom floor, the Colonel commanded, "Sir, let's take refuge there!"

They ran into a bunker at the port, "Now what?" Marco asked.

"Lieutenant?" asked Colonel Gustave on the radio, "Those damn cyborg, we'll need the guillotine after this — to removing their useless brain and use their bodies parts."

But the lieutenant did not answer, so the Colonel walked out alone.

Shortly, Marco, who was confused, sat waiting at the bunker. Suddenly an explosion occurred — this time from the airport located on the middle floor. Marco saw a lot of debris falling, including a plane. Alexa then controlled the flight and took it to Marco.

Colonel Gustave came back and said, "Let's just take the boat." Then he saw Marco's plane already there and said, "Sir, forget that—the plane is better."

The civilian ships that were there had been transformed into battleships by Colonel Gustave. Equipped with broad arrows with an explosive tip and several canon weapons, their warship shot more STARS transport aircraft.

When Marco was about to board his plane, Alexa controlled the flight and flew into the air, saying, "No, Monsieur, let me clear the line alone."

Alexa controlled the plane alone and shot many Spacejet STARS in the sky.

"Then why do you need a pilot? Take your other plane out again," Marco said irritably because Alexa took his plane.

Alexa replied, "I have only two, and they will be saved for others if you fail."

Marco said angrily, "They? In one hundred years, only two people could meet you; you might need another fifty years for one person to make it to the planet. And also, I am sure the Dragon that lives on this planet will get stronger. Trust me, let's make total war. No more waiting!"

Alexa then returned the plane to Marco. He said, "Okay Monsieur Marco, I will bring my other plane."

"Good, very good. Finally, you become more useful," Marco answered.

Marco then flew his own plane, which was advanced enough to be able to defeat the STARS spacejet which was more damaged and poorly maintained. Shortly, the most massive Eiffel tower was destroyed by STARS and collapsed down into the water while destroying the port below.

Passing through many tall towers that stood above the clouds, the city of Rivière looked beautiful even though it was dead. "Alexa," Marco asked, "This place is wonderful! Was this a kind of tourist place a hundred years ago?"

"Yes," Alexa answered briefly.

Suddenly lots of Spacejet and STARS Aircraft began to chase Marco, while Alexa's plane was still on its way to it. Marco tried to fly in and out of the towers and hot air balloons while dangerously tricking the enemy. Colonel Gustave's forces tried to shoot the STARS aircraft, and it helped a little. Some Spacejet STARS ran out of energy fuel and then fell down by themselves, and some were shot by Gustave's troops. But their numbers were increasing and chasing Marco. While trying to dodge STARS attacks, Marco flew low past Gustave's battleships, and the ship managed to also shoot many STARS planes. A STARS plane appeared from behind to ambush Marco but ran out of bullets and then tried to hit him, but Marco dodged quickly, so the plane crashed into a ship.

"Hahaha, this is very exciting!" Marco said with enthusiasm. "But it's a little scary. I like that."

Unexpectedly, a Grande submarine emerged from the water; however, the sub had been stolen by STARS, and from the water, they tried to shoot many towers where Gustave's troops stayed. Their torpedo shots flew out, hitting many poles under the foot of the tower.

"Monsieur, I still need a few minutes to get there. Please help Gustave's troops and shoot the STARS submarine," Alexa said via video call.

Marco answered doubtfully, "But I can't see them. The submarine is quite advanced, so they're not visible on my radar."

"Enter into the water and use sonar," said Alexa.

"OK, okay," Marco said, then flew his plane into the water

without hesitation and searched for the STARS submarine.

Apparently, there were many submarines in the water, so he needed many shots in the water. Many submarine positions were known, and Gustave's ships assisted in shooting them with their ship torpedo.

"Nice, Monsieur, stay in the water so the spacejet STARS can't track you," Alexa said, praising him.

"What is the name of my plane?" Marco asked.

Alexa answered, "Chasseur; I also like to call it Sea Bird."

"Pretty good," said Marco "For jet craft produced a hundred years ago."

STARS began to be overwhelmed by being in the middle of the defense of Colonel Gustave's forces, and the rest of their troops began to focus solely on Marco. There were many turrets in hundreds of tall towers and battleships, and the airplanes of Colonel Gustave finally were able to beat the STARS air strikes one by one. Some STARS spacejets managed to track Marco and enter the water. Of the many Spacejet STARS that went into the water, only a few were not damaged; most of the aircraft that were in poor condition just patrolled in the air while shooting at Marco who was underwater. As he accelerated the plane, Marco came out of the water and arrived at the beach on the river bank, and there was a pretty big city. The city called Nightblue was located on the border between the countries of La Grande République and the Federation of Victorieux in the South. Victorieux was a colonial country with a mixture of France and Germany.

"What are you doing?" Alexa said "Back in line."

"I have tried, but too many STARS spacejets are chasing me," Marco answered in a shaking voice.

With a somewhat weak tone, Alexa said, "No, Monsieur, that's the territory of the southern countries. You are already outside the Grande Country jurisdiction."

"I have been there quietly; the place was very dead, and I have often practiced bombarding the place without seeing any meaningful defense," Marco said.

Alexa answered, "Monsieur, you have triggered a war that had stopped a hundred years ago between the northern countries and the southern countries."

* * *

Marco tried to spin, but because of the speed of his plane, he began to turn too far into the territory of the South. With many STARS spacejets chasing, an AI defense system in the Victorieux Federation — which is one of the countries on the border — began to be active again because it thought their country was being attacked by the Grande Military. Several airwaves from joint forces from southern states started to appear. The first wave of AI-controlled Federation Victorieux air defense began to appear in the sky, flown from one of their closest air bases while Marco's plane was too far from Colonel Gustave's robot troops, so he had to be able to save himself. Marco began to use Victoire's air raid as a referee because the Spacejet STARS fighter who was chasing him looked more dangerous and he flew into the ranks of Victoire's army. Seeing the Spacejet STARS chasing him without retreating, Marco found hundreds of dark purple Victoire airplanes in the sky and clouds. There were also many large Victoire transport planes that contained many small unmanned aircraft. Victoire's small planes started coming out to attack Marco and the STARS Spacejet. Trying to deceive while circling behind the big STARS planes, Marco was targeted from all directions by several of Victoire's fixed planes moving forward, and the line seemed to not stop moving forward to the area of the Grande country.

"What are you doing?" Asked Alexa to Marco by phone.

Being busy, looking for a gap to escape, Marco did not answer. He then tried to turn around but was swarmed by Victoire's airplanes; several large Victoire planes tried to shoot Marco, but because of the slower speed of their aircraft, their shots started to hit other Victoire planes around. STARS Spacejet began to scatter, but some were still able to catch Marco, and some even cut the lane and found Marco's position and tried to shoot him. Marco's spacejet had an energy-shielding system which seemed to not last forever; some Victoire fighter jets began to chase them, too, making things even crazier for Marco.

Marco called Alexa and asked for help with a trembling voice, "Hello, Alexa, are there any suggestions?"

Alexa replied, "Oh, now you talk. Spin northward somehow; there is Grande's air defense system that is ready to shoot anyone. Try to get there and get out of the Southern country — it is hazardous to be in there."

"OK, I'll try it" Marco answered.

Then there was a fighter that caught Marco's attention; the plane was from Victoire's army and colored in yellow. The yellow plane quickly shot several weak Spacejet STARS that chased Marco and dropped two of them from behind. Then the yellow plane similar to Marco's plane chased him.

"Alexa," Marco said nervously, "Who is this Victoire's yellow spacejet that chasing me?"

Alexa answered in a low tone, she said, "Yellow plane? They named it the Blonde; the plane was driven by a very dangerous female pilot from the Federation country of Victorieux, a small, impoverished country with a mixture of French-German from the South. But that was from a hundred years ago."

The yellow plane then chased Marco quickly; several times Marco tried to lose it, but failed. Strangely the yellow plane did not shoot at Marco at all.

Maybe her bullets are empty? Marco thought.

Inevitably, the well-maintained yellow plane approached Marco's plane from the side, and Marco saw through the window that there was a yellow-haired pilot.

Oh, again a corpse, Marco thought tensely.

Curious, Marco tried to let her closer, after seeing the pilot on the yellow plane from the side; the pilot began turning her head to see Marco.

"HAH? GHOST OR ROBOT?" Marco shouted, feeling surprised at himself, and then drove the plane away from there because he was afraid.

But the yellow plane kept approaching as if she wanted to talk. They are high enough so that they are far from other aircraft. Marco brought his plane closer to Victoire's yellow plane. The second plane then passed through the storm clouds and enters bright sunlight above. Unable to contact each other because of the Firewall radio system, Marco tried to wave his hand; surprisingly, the yellow pilot also waved her hands. The pilot was seen wearing a helm so he could not know whether it was a robot or not.

"Alexa," asked Marco via video call. "Does this pilot look alive? You say everyone is dead; is she like you? The one where only human memory is stored in AI's robot brain?"

Alexa replied "Ah bon? I don't know Monsieur. The Victorieux Federation is a poor country that we often destroy; sorry. First, there is no way they have such technology, or maybe they got it from another larger southern country. I will turn off the Firewall's communication so you can talk to her. Okay?"

"Do it, Alexa," Marco ordered enthusiastically.

After the Firewall was turned off, Marco began trying to talk to the yellow pilot via the sound radio. "Hello, hello," Marco said.

The pilot did not answer in a voice but with something like

Germanic-language dance song was sent to Marco. Feeling confused, Marco said again in a joking tone, "Sorry, I don't know your language. Can you speak Modern English? French? Are you an AI or a ghost?"

Several STARS spacejets were seen from behind quickly approaching and cut off their conversation.

Because there is no Firewall, a STARS pilot robot speaks in a robotic voice saying "Attention citizen, don't move! Loser!"

The yellow plane then shot the STARS plane with a machine gun in the bottom of her plane, destroying one of the STARS planes and killing the pilot. The Spacejet STARS then flew without direction to the wind. Marco looked carefully at what was going to happen, the STARS plane then went up too high through the atmosphere and was suddenly destroyed by a powerful lightning attack that turned it to ash.

"Ouch," Marco said reacting.

Because there were two powerful planes in front, the rest of the other STARS spacejets then chose to retreat and were no longer visible. When Marco saw that no one was following them from behind, the pilot on the yellow plane then delivered a hand signal indicating Marco to land. He agreed and the two went flying down through the clouds and reached a rocky mountain. The pilot landed the yellow plane on the tall, black, rocky mountain and Marco landed his plane beside her. The place looked bright and windy because it was above a storm cloud with little oxygen. Marco turned from his plane while not releasing the helm; the pilot woman also went down, and the woman did not look thin like a Corpse or a robot.

Preparing his mind to meet strangers, Marco advanced and said "Hello, Miss. Nice to meet you."

The women then opened her helmet. She looked like a human with body shapes and faces that don't look like corpses nor robots. She didn't speak anything yet.

"Can you speak Modern English?" Marco asked.

"Yes," she answered.

Continuing, Marco asked, "Are you a human or a robot?"

The woman answered "I'm not really sure. Who are you?"

"Hah? I am human, one hundred percent, but not from this planet. My name is Marco." He answered enthusiastically.

"Good," she replied. "At least you are still alive."

Marco then thought that the woman was only an AI that was lifted from the memory of the human brain. *She's a Replica.*

The woman looked at Marco with a pessimistic look and asked, "You look happy; is this like a vacation for you?"

Marco's face fell; he was nervous and said honestly, "No, I'm actually terrified, very scared, surrounded by death, and I'm just trying to be strong even though in my heart . . . ah, forget it, I think you know. I might be the only survivor of my friends."

The woman answered, "Don't lose hope." Then the woman said, "Jump to the point; what are you doing here?"

Marco answered, standing straight while pointing his forefinger at her repeatedly, "To fight the Dragon who killed my friend, your friend, my enemy, your enemy, and maybe later me or perhaps it also killed you."

"So you're trapped just like us," she said, "You can't do it alone."

CHAPTER 8

Marco said to her "I have been assisted by Alexa—do you know her? Some robots from the southern Grande province of Grande also helped, namely Colonel Gustave."

The woman did not reply, so Marco continued, asking, "Where are you living? Are you Android from Central?"

The woman advanced to hold Marco's face several times and backed away saying, "Warm skin, I like that. Why do I stay alive? I died a hundred years ago, now all you see is a replica of a robot with the help of the AI brain that came from my memory that was moved. I am only a lifeless person, and animated. I am not an Android from Central, I only wear an Android body that resembles a human, put to sleep for a hundred years waiting for something to arouse us, and you appeared to bombard our country yesterday."

"What can I say? I'm interested in the history of this place," Marco said.

The woman replied, "Dragon's energy waves quickly spread, Phoenix controlled the atmosphere, and the best troops were gathered by the southern countries. I was one of the chosen. When my memory was lifted, I became lifeless or dead. Several other people tried to hide inside the ground; others tried to freeze themselves, shrinking their heartbeats, making themselves faint, but in the end, everyone died because of the dragon's energy waves that passed through the entire planet. Only few robots and AI were left. The UW fleet tried to help but continued to fail, and finally, the planet was sold to a researcher like Central for experiments. They are holding the Dragon out of here."

"That's ridiculous," Marco said, "Why didn't UW and Central just come down to help bombard the Dragons?"

She replied, "To destroy a Dragon, they need extraordinarily strong energy, so that the Dragon's fully-energized body cannot resist and it becomes overloaded. But weapons like that cost money, energy, and time. So they chose to leave this planet like this while conserving it to look for better weapons."

"You know a lot. I'm sorry to hear that," Marco said.

Said the woman, "Please don't remind me again about what happened here; lots of replicas were not ready and committed suicide afterward, they're all just a bunch of broken animatronics. Don't remind me that everyone I know and myself are dead. It's unfortunate—you don't know how painful it is to cry but can shed no tears."

Taking a deep breath, Marco said, "Join me! Together we will defeat the Dragon and attack the center of their heart on the mountain!"

"First of all," replied the woman. "You must be able to unite all the forces on this planet. Grande's military strength that is left alone is not enough; look for other powers from northern countries and southern countries. Their defenses are now only controlled by AI, and some AIs are useless. So you have to be able to reset and persuade others."

"Good, where do you start?" Marco asked.

The woman answered, "From a small country. Federation Victorieux is a small country, so you have to reset and re-upload AI brains from our defense system. As you can see, they continue to send troops as if there were still world wars, without realizing everyone is dead."

"Wait a minute," Marco said.

Marco tried to contact Alexa and said, "Alexa, I found a new friend; they look sane and want to help us. The Victorieux Federation seems to have some Androids with human memories or Replicas."

Alexa replied quickly, saying, "Hein? Do what you need to do, Monsieur, but be careful. I can't help up close because the control distance of my plane is limited. Stop Victoire's military attack before the remaining troops from Colonel Gustave are destroyed."

Marco looked at his new friend, who said in a strong voice, "Call me Lisa. Let's go attack my own headquarters commando. We'll reset the AI there so that it can be controlled."

"Are we two enough?" Marco asked.

"Enough," she answered.

Then Marco asked again "What is the plan when we arrive?"

Lisa said, "The AI in the command center doesn't let anyone close, so you turn their attention in the air while I fly in. Sorry, but I can't turn off my Firewall, so I can't receive messages from you—I can only send messages."

The two then boarded their own planes and flew into the sky. While following Lisa's plane, Marco headed to a place he did not know, passed through the storm clouds, and reached the dark world below again. Lisa took him through an area that was not awake, while crossing a shortcut—both of them finally reached a military base in the middle of a flat desert without life.

Another valley of death, Marco thought.

Then he received a voicemail from Lisa that said: "Marco, this is a restricted area for flights so we both will be shot at; divert AA's gun attention, and I will try to enter their gate. Hopefully, the Victoire AI system can be turned off, and I can wake up other Replicas."

Marco headed straight up while bombarding and shooting rockets at the headquarters walls. Seeing the light of the fire from a turret shot like rain rising to the sky toward Marco, Lisa advanced in another direction while shooting and entered into a runway tunnel successfully. Many Marsouin Victoire robots came out trying to kill Lisa, but she was able to dodge them in a narrow hallway with her Spacejet. The passageway in the base was large enough so her spacejet could enter; Lisa remained in the center of the Headquarters inside large, dark, lifeless buildings. There were also many airplanes and vehicles parked in the area. Some Victory jet fighters finally came out from several runways, controlled by AI from the Victoire command center tower deep in the underground. Victoire fighter jets then chased Marco, who tried to avoid them while circling above Headquarters. He couldn't be too fast because it would keep him away and no longer act as bait. He was lucky because many turrets were inactive, which made Marco's plane movements even more out of fire range.

"I have entered the command center," said Lisa.

Hearing that, Marco turned the plane into the tunnel while continuing to be chased by many Victoire warplanes. Lisa got off her plane and entered one of several doors in the command center, going deeper into the underground. Marco pursued with his plane but became confused because of the many aisles in the Headquarters. He then turned his plane abruptly and shot Victoire's fighter planes which had chased him down the aisle where it was clogged by a destroyed aircraft. He tried to shoot the roof, but instead, the ground and buildings collapsed. Feeling trapped with his plane, Marco decided to go on foot. The place was very dark, so he had to continue to wear a helm that had special night goggles, and there were flashlights from the approaching Marsouin Victoire robots.

"Alexa," Marco said by phone "Please control my plane."

But there was no response from Alexa because the distance of the control was too far due to the number of satellites and the connecting system that were not functioning anymore. Feeling better on the plane, Marco went back up and shot the place with aircraft engine guns and caused the walls to fall apart. Many Victoire fighter jets tried to chase Marco, but the place to enter the site had been blocked by debris. While Lisa kept coming in, she didn't stop shooting many AI-controlled Marsouin robots from the computer in Victoire's command center. Lisa came in and got a small door when she approached many Marsouin robots coming out of it, then she continued to shoot them, so the robots were destroyed and piled up like a hill on the small door. When all was clogged, Lisa threw a grenade and blew up the place to make way for her. After walking farther away, more Marsouin robots sprang up with some dangerous small drones.

"Marco, come quickly to my position. I am near the entrance to the command center, "Lisa said on the radio.

Marco could not answer it but could only hear, so he decided to find a way to Lisa. Lisa then sent some significant coordinates to Marco, who looked for a shortcut by shooting many walls and then barging in.

What am I doing? Marco thought—getting many dead ends, but he still shot and destroyed the wall to open the shortcut with his plane.

Lisa became cornered, and then ran back to protect herself anywhere that she could, but was finally really trapped with a large wall behind her. While trying to shoot her own troops chasing him, suddenly Marco appeared with his plane through the hole in the wall he had destroyed. Lisa looked down while watching Marco shoot the enemies of the robots in that place. Then Marco advanced, flying low with his plane forward inside the underground tunnel, while Lisa followed him from behind with foot.

"A pilot can't leave his plane," Marco taunted, as the speaker mocked Lisa, who had left her plane behind.

Small AI-controlled troops from Victoire's command center were overwhelmed by being too weak to face an advanced fighter that entered their rooms. Marco shot many EMP rockets into the rooms there and turned off many turrets as well as robots. Inside the dark hall, as the blue eye rays of Victoire's robots made their positions visible, Marco and Lisa quickly entered deeper into Victoire's headquarters. Because of the narrow room, Marco decided to go on foot and activated the auto-pilot where the plane would shoot on its own while acting like a turret. Marco and Lisa then entered together. After descending the steps, they arrived at a small hallway leading to the command center, with many computers and monitors on the side. After they walked almost to the end of the hall, someone else stood up—another Replica blocked them. The replica was one of the soldiers who woke up, fully clothed with weapons, and he stood up without saying anything. The man was likely confused and sad knowing the whole planet was dead.

* * *

"Take it easy," said Lisa "We pass him slowly."

Then Marco and Lisa walked past the man who stood like a statue. They arrived at the control center room, seeing that the AI computer engine was still functioning thanks to the electricity reserves from military nuclear batteries and windmills around the base. Lisa then quickly headed for one of the main computers.

Marco said "Wait, do you know how to use it? Do you know the password?"

"No need. Replica is the password; it is me" Lisa answered while using the computer.

For a while, the computer AI command center became passive and could be controlled. Lisa tried to restore the other Replicas to wake up from their sleep on Victorieux base; even the country did not have a lot of Replicas.

"Scheisse! Not enough pilots," said Lisa angrily. "We have to go to the other command center and wake everyone up. I mean Replicas that are still sleeping in other cities.

Some of the replicas that are there are pilots, scientists, and some other famous political people. They all came together in a large conference room nearby, where they began to talk a lot to one another. Suddenly Lisa showed up with Marco on a forum; Marco was dressed in the Grande army and everyone there was quietly watching him.

Lisa then spoke to them all loudly: "WELCOME BACK, BROTHERS AND SISTERS! The time has come. Don't think about negative things. Now that we have slept for a hundred years, we are new people; the old world has long gone, and we must forget it because everything has passed. Sad advice, but you have to forget your old name and use a new one. Stop remembering the past — it will only make you sad."

A Replica person raised his hand and asked, "What happened here?"

Lisa answered him, "I don't have much time to explain; you have to find it yourself. I woke up a day before and got an important mission to avenge the death of our planet."

"So the wave of Dragon's energy really killed everyone?" said another Replica.

Then some of them became sad; others became angry and hysterical. Many replicas were sitting quietly on the floor, but there were some who were willing to follow Lisa. The two most difficult events after the resurrection, which lost themselves and everything. With feelings formed from the logic of the robot's brain, they have difficulty expressing themselves, due to the lack of biological, emotional elements in the robot's body. A person who is reborn with no heaven but a dreamless life.

"They need a little time," Lisa said to Marco,

Marco asked, "Have you been crying the whole time you

were here?"

Lisa did not answer. Without wasting time, they commanded Victoire's air forces which had been controlled by a computer AI to return to headquarters. Lisa and Marco then drew up the next plan with some conscious replicas. Most of them try to wonder, trying to convince themselves that they were human before, but were not. They are just replicas with stolen memories. Lisa tried to convince the spirit of their hearts made of metal. Getting awareness — and accepting who we are — is the hardest thing that must be able to make us confident.

"We divide the group," said Lisa. "Some will split into other command locations in the South to wake everyone up at once."

They formed a team of three to four people to go to every southern country.

Lisa saw that, one by one, as the most influential military pilot in her country, they heard her. She said "Come on, we will revive a strong alliance of the Australis Army, not to attack northern countries but to attack the true enemy of mankind, Dragon. Gather together alliances; each of your groups is going to other southern countries, namely: Rozenland, New Athen, Redland, Perseus, Virginia, Kingdom of New Alps, Svesland and other countries."

A Replica asked Lisa, "Madam, we understand very well for the communion of the southern state, our alliance of Australium, but what about the Septentrions alliance in the north? There are seven big countries in the north, can they be friends?"

"I leave it to Marco," Lisa answered.

Marco is shocked but agrees, "Yes, I have many friends in one of the northern countries, Grande — maybe they can help; after all, your war ended a hundred years ago, right? We all are friends now."

"Prima! Das ist prima, but Listen, Marco," said Lisa. "Some northern hemisphere countries have never been touched by war, so they are powerful; some of them are Nordic-speaking, New Dutch-speaking countries, and other northern countries that I have forgotten. During the war, the south was larger but fragmented. Northern was wealthy because of using our natural resources. But we have forgotten that, so they must have forgotten it, too. You have to go there, meet all North Replicas and convince them to join us . . . but be careful. Don't be a besserwisser."

"Besser . . . what?" Marco asked, confused.

"Oh, never mind," Lisa answered.

* * *

The Victorieux Federation self-defense AI has fallen into their hands, and the Marsouin robots and other AI systems have returned to normal. Lisa then reopened the base. Marco could now board his plane and return to Grande as a representative. After flying over the border, the situation seemed calm between the Federation States of Victorieux and the Southern Province of Grande. No STARS or shots were approaching from the land. Marco returned to Colonel Gustave's place; he found they were still waiting for him, watching from the Barrage as their ship still remained motionless.

"Hello, Alexa," Marco said, "I have returned."

Alexa answered by phone. "Merveilleux! Monsieur, I know what you mean. The Victorieux Federation has returned and wrote to me about your plan. I strongly agree, and we have prepared your journey to the far north."

"I will stop at your place; my energy and ammunition have run out," Marco said.

Alexa replied "Unfortunately, you have to use another plane. My tower is being beaten by STARS, and I am busy shooting at them now—with help from my Chasseur spacejet and some robotic forces from Colonel Gustave."

"Where should I land?" Marco asked, then got the direction of the landing from Alexa, to a runway near the port close to the destroyed Eiffel tower.

After landing, Marco got off the plane. He met Colonel Gustavo again; this time the colonel suggested that Marco use one of his ships.

Another robot said, "Monsieur, everyone has been waiting for your arrival; as instructed by Captain Alexa, we will go down into the territory of northern countries using ships so as not to invite the arrival of STARS troops who control the city of Grande. We smuggle our airplanes in ships so as not to be suspicious."

"All right, Colonel, please keep and guard my plane here, because it's running out of everything," Marco ordered.

"I'm ready to host my hero!" replied the Colonel.

CHAPTER 9

Marco was transported on a large tourist cruiser which was modified into a battleship by Gustave's forces. Inside the ship, many airplanes would be used when they cross the Grande border which is controlled by STARS Ranger robots. Hundreds of ships from small to large sizes like boat and yacht were passed over the big river and out through the sea. There were no planes in the air other than small surveillance drones; all transport planes, fighter jets, and military vehicles were loaded into ships. They sailed through the western province of Grande, namely Lone Island province. Only a few robotic troops corps were taken down to the island; the rest continued to sail north, and, after one day passing through the cities of Grande without the knowledge of STARS troops, they finally arrived at a border area. After traveling through the sea from the side of the Grande continent, they came to a North European-speaking country in the north called Wonderland; the city buildings were in Victorian architecture the same as in the Victorieux country — 1800s-era buildings. In the middle of the city, there was a large palace and a statue of Constantine their leader as high as a thousand meters above the mountain. There was a palace on the top of the mountain, surrounded by five layers of gold-colored walls as high as one hundred meters, dense and three kilometers between the walls filled with many buildings on the ground.

"Look, sir, once, the country was filled with gold mines and became the center of world trade," Gustavo said to Marco while showing his robot finger towards the horizon.

He continued "We are far from STARS headquarters; sorry. Our ship is not too fast because it is only a modified civilian ship. Now we will use airplanes to be faster."

Marco said, "You are smart enough for an ordinary robot—you sure you're not a Replica?"

The robot colonel replied, "No, but thank you, sir. I have learned to fight Ranger robots for decades on this planet, so I know very well what they are thinking."

Marco boarded a big passenger plane and was escorted by many other air fighters as they flew into the remaining Wonderland country. From the sky it looked like the city of the country was so beautiful, and the yellowish-red moonlight illuminated the nation's capital, making the buildings glow in gold and white. They get lots of colorful balloons and festivals there.

Marco then asked the Colonel, who was sitting beside him, "Colonel, why is this city so beautiful and not crushed like the others?"

The robot colonel tried to answer him. "Sir, this is where all the trees in the north have gone; remaining Replicas built this city from recycling the planet's metal and trees. Wonderland is very rich, the center of world trade, in the most northern region and untouched by war. That was why this place didn't seem destroyed even though all humans had died by the Dragon's energy wave a hundred years ago. It is also the last city to be hit by a wave of energy so there may be many replicas from civilian survivors here."

Wonderland Air Defense let Gustave's airplane enter because they used the Grande logo which was an ally of northern countries. They then landed at the airport at the edge of the sea. Marco and the others got off their planes while other aircraft remained to patrol the air. Marco's eyes were shocked to see the many robots and replicas that walked there like there wasn't any war. On the runway, they were greeted by several canned-faced Robots from Wonderland who were dressed as a royal — in red, gold-plated cloth, with a tall, red hat. A wonderful place, everything looks crafted in such a way to be pleasing to the eye for desperate people, to make everyone forget all their nightmares for a moment.

"Welcome to Sagoland, a cloud cuckoo land from the north! Say the purpose and who you are," said a butler robot there who welcomed Marco's arrival.

Replica robots largely there have been given the various drugs or fluids strange to tranquilizers.

Colonel Gustave answered, "Hello, canned face, I want to meet your leader. We are from your neighboring Grande country."

"Once again, welcome to Sagoland! Come with me," said the greeting robot while leading them to a large classic car.

Marco was still surprised to see the place. He said, "Colonel, see, they have protected this place all this time. Extraordinary."

He got a phone call from Alexa, it turns out that their satellite was functioning correctly in the northern countries. Alexa said to Marco, "Monsieur, still be careful. The Wonderland country has been isolated so far. I don't know what happened there. But don't worry because they are also part of the Septentriones Confederation or seven stars from the north."

"Take it easy," replied Marco. "This place looks friendly and beautiful. I need this to relieve my depression."

* * *

During the trip, they encountered many replicas and ordinary robots running along the highway in the city, and everything looked very healthy — like nothing terrible had happened to the planet. There was no storm on the planet's North Pole so the weather seemed bright during the day and night and remains the same. With lots of cars, the convoy arrived shortly at a mayor's building, one of the essential buildings in the city located near the second wall. There was a big green lawn park in front of the building. Marco was interested because he hadn't seen anything green for a long time. After getting out of the car, they have all ushered up a staircase to the gate of the mayor's building. All weapons requested were handed over, but Gustave's group did not want to. When they entered, all of them were allowed to sit at the long table's right in front of the large entrance. No one looked suspicious or worried; in fact, everyone seemed cheerful. Someone came down from the top floor to find them. He was the Mayor of Wonderland, Mr. Saint Constantine, an old man who was well-dressed and wearing a bow tie; his face was full of white hair, and he was a Replica. Marco and Colonel Gustave also sat at chairs at the long table.

Some robotic servants came with food. "Oh, I hope this time it's not rotten food and fish bones," Marco said, looking at Colonel Gustave.

It proved to be factory-made food with much fake meat and fake vegetables. Marco chose not to eat it even though his mouth was watering.

Said the Wonderland Mayor who came to them, "Welcome master and robots to our beautiful city with Steam, Wind, Solar and Cyber technology. After all, we haven't had a guest for a long time; the king wants to meet you."

"King?" Marco asked.

The mayor replied, "Yes, and I am the person. I'm Saint Constantine. Hohohoho . . ."

Colonel Gustave did not want to talk much and said, "Sorry, sir, and thank you for the welcome but we . . ."

The mayor stopped his statement; after that, Constantine

said, "I know your destination."

"That's great, then," Marco said. "Tell us where your troops are, and we will gather all the power on this planet and attack Dragon."

"No, don't attack Dragon," said Saint Constantine.

"Why?" Marco asked.

He replied "Why? Look at what happened to the great city of Grande, when they let a human named Lee ten years ago try to attack Phoenix! Grande was strong, but how crazy it was. The Phoenix attacked back, and the whole military of Grande was destroyed. Now, Grande is controlled by STARS. Only what remains is from the southern province where the Colonel came from."

Marco said, "You can't hide forever from a Dragon; someday they will rise fully again. But if you want to be a loser, then that is your choice, and we will get out of this clown country."

Said Saint Constantine again. "Listen! It's taken a hundred years to rebuild this country. Replicas in the northern countries have gotten up early, while all Replicas from Southern countries were still asleep. We have more experience—we know our choices. When the Grande was destroyed ten years ago because it was about to destroy peace, many Replicas from other countries joined us. We have the best defense system and are untouched by STARS."

"Yes, thank you for the welcome sir," Colonel Gustave said, agreeing to Marco's words as he stood about to leave the room.

Seeing them going to leave, Mr. Saint Constantine tried to stop them and said, "Oh, I'm just joking. Stay in your chair!"

"Oh, you want to meet him after all, what do you say?" Colonel Gustave asked innocently.

Marco, becoming paranoid, said, "Your words are too serious to be made a joke. It is not funny."

One of Gustave's planes was shot and heard outside. Those in the building panicked and ran looking out. Gustave saw one of his aircraft crashed into the park.

"Sir, what is this? Who shot my plane?!" Gustave said in the tone of his angry robot.

"NO ONE MOVES!" Constantine shouted to them. "I will not let you destroy the peace that Dragon has given us for a hundred years. We can study Dragon to defeat them but not now. Think about it—you attack them, then they will be angry and kill everyone again!"

Marco looked at him angrily and said, "No, you can't stop us, since the Dragon should have been defeated a long time ago. You just shut up! A hundred years! Think about all the humans who have died."

"No, not Mr. Marco," Constantine said, "I know you just want to go home and don't want to die on this planet."

Alexa then spoke past a speaker through one of Gustave's robots. "And that spirit is what I need."

Knowing that voice, Constantine said, "Oh, so you are Miss Alexa. I thought you were dead ten years ago."

Alexa said, "Hey, coward, you guys let us fight alone so that all our replicas and robots die on Grande. How long will you hide, Constantine? The dragon has become stronger and has gathered a great deal of energy from the sun! Marco, don't listen to him, get out of there."

Marco looked again at Constantine about to lift his gun and said "Sir, you seem too afraid to die for twice. After all, isn't your age two hundred years? Twice the normal human life."

Seeing that Marco could not be persuaded, Saint Constantine said to his people, "Listen my children, the Replicas and Robots! This man is not part of us. The Replicas hear! We are new people; we aren't from the past, and we have a new home, a new life, and a beautiful world that we can build together! This man just wants to go home, he doesn't care about the planet!"

"YOU'RE WRONG, SIR," Marco shouted. "I am a hero who will liberate this place and avenge the deaths of those who have fallen a hundred years ago."

Colonel Gustave said "That's right, sir, even though it's just an ordinary robot and not a replica of past human memories. I had died before being brought back by Alexa—unlike before where I was killed in a state of ignorance by waves of energy, this time I will die in battle!"

Saint Constantine looked behind him and said to his man, "Hey, you, send Fredsbevarer troops! My Hjalmar! My Ansgar Knight!"

Then there appeared lots of Replica from men and women with human faces, in army uniforms with fancy royal clothing in classic style and in red cloth. While wearing great helm of steel plates and heavy long spear, they began to ambush some of Colonel Gustave's green Marsouin robots there.

"The troops have appeared; what should we do, Colonel?" Marco asked.

The colonel replied, "Sir, that is Fred's' guard, or we usually call him Freddy Knight. They are replicas that have been brainwashed by Mr. Saint Constantine."

"Yes, but what now?" Marco asked again, feeling confused.

Turning to look at Marco, the Colonel answered "Opposite, we are their opponents, sir."

Then Marco looked at Constantine who was standing right in front of them and said "Don't move! I'll catch you!"

Saint Constantine laughed. "Catch? Can you catch a hologram? Hohohoho . . . "

Marco then tried to shoot him, but the bullet passed through the body of Saint Constantine like in air because he was only a hologram. A Replica that is just a hologram-like Alexa.

Marco and Gustave were about to walk out, but the hologram of Saint Constantine appeared again in front of them and said, "I am a god in Wonderland; no matter wherever you go, I will get you! Give up you idiot."

But Marco and Gustave walked past the hologram—like they

didn't care. Freddy's troops then started shooting at them all with weapons; the Special Forces trapped and hunted Gustave's Marsouin robots. They were right in the middle of the city, feeling cornered, Colonel Gustave asking for air help but no one could get close. All the planes were shot by the Wonderland canon forces controlled by Constantine. Many cars and Cavalry troops from Constantine were seen filling the gate near the park. Cavalries were coming in using robotic horses decorated with a red cloth like kingdom knight.

"Sir, let's retreat!" Gustave said as he walked back inside the building.

When he and Marco were about to get cover inside, the doors began to open and more and more Police Robotic troops named Santarmi came out to attack them, while Freddy's forces who were human Replicas were at the back of the line.

Seeing the situation getting worse, Gustave ordered "Sir, take refuge; I will order my troops to detonate themselves."

"What?" Marco asked, confused.

Gustave's Marsouin robots then blew themselves apart making the line of Constantine's Santarmi robots a mess.

Constantine's hologram reappeared in their midst; he said a lot while they continued to be attacked. Finally, he said, "Gentlemen, please stop this violence. I won't let you attack the Dragon—it will make the planet break again like it used to!"

"Be quiet, Santa," said Gustave. "We have been waiting for quite a while. I can't wait to hit them. Don't side with the enemy."

Constantine said, "Gent, give me more time. We are not ready, what's wrong with living in peace with Dragon? Have some consensus with us; in our culture, we must try to minimize conflicts. There must be a solution between us. I can't let you make the heaven that I woke with difficulty be destroyed, because the Dragon is too strong for you."

Colonel Gustave and Marco did not pay attention to the

words of Constantine. They went to try to survive the onslaught of Constantine's inexhaustible robots. Many pieces of metal and iron flew everywhere; the place looked messy with a robotic body that broke out because it was hit and exploded. The floors of the white building were now filled with oil and metal. There were large columns in the building. Marco tried to protect himself, but his condition began to worsen.

"SIR, WE HAVE TO GET OUT OF HERE!" Gustave shouted in his robotic voice.

"Get out?" Marco's reaction confused the colonel; he said in a panic, "But there are more enemies out there!"

Alexa then contacted them after seeing the incident through the camera. "Monsieur, your pilot's clothes can be used to fly, use them and get to the right side of the building — there is a small window there."

"Can you fly?" Marco asked Gustave.

Gustave answered, "Oh, fly? No, you get out to save yourself. I will hold their attention."

Some Constantine Replicas named Freddy's forces then appeared in small, powerful Mecha armor and attacked Marco. With no choice, finally Marco decided to fly out of the building through a window with his jet-suit. Gustave followed him from behind by foot. The entire building was now controlled by Constantine's robotic forces so that those who remained must walk out to a large park. The park that circled the building was vast, with the building in the middle. The park was surrounded by a tall white fence that was closed. The city was made with a touch of stunning art — made with aesthetic reasons — but the main reason was an escape from reality. Replicas in Wonderland have been controlled by Constantine, with his idea of self-love and a momentary false dream.

When all Gustave's troops came out, he called his ship's artillery. "Soldiers! Shoot this building!"

Without asking, the Gustave ships controlled by the robotic

forces immediately shot at the Mayor's building. The entire Constantine robot army inside was destroyed and that made Constantine angry. Freddy's knights managed to get out of the explosion, while the whole park was still controlled by Constantine's Santarmi robots. Freddy's horsemen also appeared, jumping between plastic flowers and garden plastic grass. Freddy rode and then used the weapon that could shoot Marco and Gustave from a distance. When Freddy rode closer, they pulled out a long and sharp electric spear. Surrounded by lots of Replicas and Constantine's Robots. Marco and Gustave tried to run and hide behind the garden walls. There was a shootout and an explosion that made the park burn. Plastic plants began to burn and the plastic flowers in the garden started to melt in color.

While running to protect himself, Marco then said to Gustave on the radio, "Colonel, how do we get out of this plastic park? Any other suggestions?"

"Calm down, sir, my men will shoot from the sea!" Then Gustave called his robots on board. "Soldiers! Shots of more artillery but smaller ones and types of fire bullets. We burn this city."

In the afternoon, red moonlight began to disappear, but thick clouds came and made the sunlight reflection dimmed so that the city darkened. Gustave's ships then fired a great deal of artillery. Most of it did not penetrate the city because of its defense system, but some slipped through and burned the park. The Freddy Horse troops were consumed by the artillery fire attacks; despite being burned, they kept riding their horses while continuing to attack Marco and Gustave's position. While Gustave's forces were trapped in the sea and could not enter the heavily-guarded airway, Marco had to endure with the strength he had.

CHAPTER 10

"Colonel!" Marco was clearly flustered. "We are getting trapped; is there no other way to make your other troops come to rescue us?"

The Colonel replied, "Sir, it's too risky, I can't lose all my troops. It took me a decade to build them."

"Then what if we lose our life?" Marco asked with sweat caused by the fires burning everywhere.

The Colonel answered while he avoided the attack of Freddy's robotic horses. "What if we invite other troops?"

"Other?" Marco asked.

"Yes, sir" Gustave answered. "Look, this city is close to the border of New Paris City which is controlled by STARS forces. We bait them here."

Horse knights almost hit Marco, but he managed to dodge. Freddy's knight then circled the park again as he passed the flames along the way.

Marco said to Gustave. "Not sure, but a good idea. Bait them with your troops!"

Gustave replied, "Unfortunately, Wonderland is guarded by Constantine's traps and turrets along the border walls, so we can only feed the STARS air forces! Get ready, sir, hang in there!"

Then Gustave conveyed his intentions to Alexa and the forces. Soon, Gustave fighter planes moved to attack STARS military headquarters near the border as if it were a plane from Wonderland.

"Sir!" said Gustave who walked over to Marco with some of his robots. "We must avoid the border wall defense system to continue our journey to the port."

"Alright, let's just try to hold on, while the ships in the port attack the walls of the turret," Marco said excitedly.

The ships anchored then released more Gustave's troops through the port of Wonderland and towards the golden wall area. Gustave's robots were scattered through much of the city's land, but they escaped, thanks to the help of fire from their ships. Some city residents immediately hid in their homes, while many fled, and several civilian robots began to randomly walk while Replicas forcibly joined the military at the behest of Constantine. The Replicas then used well-developed armor and good weapons. All of them were seconded to become reserve troops of Freddy's army who were dressed in stronger forces.

Gustave's troops called him on the radio. "Colonel, the replica in the city has become a militia helping their main robotic forces. It will take more time for us to get to your position."

Alexa called Marco and Gustave as she heard that Gustave had orders to bait STARS troops from New Paris. She asked, "Monsieur, why are you dividing our troops? You can be delayed longer."

Marco answered, "Miss, we need more power. Gustave's forces here are not enough. This city is too big! We need to bait the STARS troops."

While they hid in the park, Gustave asked, "Do you like wine, sir?"

Marco was confused and didn't answer. Then Gustave, who was a robot, breathed fire through a hose from his body in the garden that was burning. Gustave's strength became stronger by heat energy, and he began to use his large machine gun that was hot with fire. Gustave shot hot-smashed bullets, like fireballs flying towards riding Freddy's knights.

"What is that?" Marco asked, lowering his head.

Gustave replied, "This is my fire bullet mixed with our oil! My artillery shots were made from the matters I needed. I call this a Greek fireball!"

A knight was hit by Gustave's fireball. The ball exploded and spilled fire oil along his body; the knight gets burnt and can't control himself, so he ran away from there and jumped in a pond in the garden, but the fire on his body was not extinguished. The knight panicked and opened his Armor, A Gustave robot hiding out in the plastic bush shot the Replica's head until it broke and died. The body of the robot fell immersed in the pool while ejecting plenty of synthetic oil in red as white smoke from its body evaporated.

Gustave saw that and laughed while saying, "Hah! Feel your second death!"

* * *

The first Replica died in that battle. Constantine became angry, and he used the incident as propaganda; a giant green hologram of his appearance appeared in the middle of the city, his hologram appearing as tall as fifty meters.

Constantine's hologram said, "Ladies and gentlemen! This is what happens if they continue to be fixated on the old world; together we protect our new world from these wicked people!"

A five-meter-diameter missile appeared from under the holographic light, the rocket flying to the hands of Constantine's hologram. He then moved as if to throw a ball at Gustave's troops, and the ball exploded when it hit the ground. This was done continuously to destroy many buildings.

"WE HAVE TO GET OUT OF THIS PARK!" Marco shouted to Gustave.

"Watch out, sir!" Gustave said. "This Park is surrounded by

walls, and above the wall, there are many turrets in the Wonderland city. We have to run out quickly!"

A Freddy warrior rode back again, emerging from black smoke from behind, and he shot while advancing, attempting to hit them with an electric spear. Gustave shot and burned him and his horse ran away and disappeared in the smoke. Suddenly, another horse knight appeared from the other direction and attacked Colonel Gustave; his electric spear hit the colonel's back. The knight went down and shot the colonel with a Carbine. Marco tried to help but had run out of bullets, then he flew with his jetsuit, hitting that Freddy until he was thrown away.

"Are you okay, Colonel?" Marco asked, looking at Gustave's condition.

"Calm, sir! I'm fine, just worry about yourself." Gustave answered.

Freddy returned, but this time he came with two other friends. The army of Gustave robots who were there then gathered together to protect their robot colonel. They shot each other, but Colonel Gustave's armor and Marco's pilot's clothes were strong enough to stop a bullet from Freddy. Freddy's forces then advanced to stab Gustave's robots with their spears, while pushing to get to Marco's position. Inside, there were flames everywhere; thick black smoke made their vision difficult while their eyes were hard to see. Gustave inhaled more fire through the hose connected to his weapon and shot everything at Freddy's direction.

"We are lucky," Marco said. "Freddy's armor is too classic; it is also made of ordinary metal, so it does not have futuristic cooling or anti-fire systems like other spacesuits today."

Unable to withstand the heat of the place, many Gustave robots became jammed, and Freddy, who caught fire, chose to retreat. While bullets from sniper fire from the walls were very disturbing, Marco continued to run out. When they arrived at the white walls, some of Freddy's snipers above him chose to jump down to the bottom. The wall was not too thick, and a Gustave robot blew himself up, destroying the wall. A stunning suicide attempt.

"SIR, I got a way out; come with me!" Gustave shouted with an active robot voice.

Marco followed his direction, and the two of them finally escaped Freddy's ambush, thanks to thick, dark smoke.

Before leaving, Marco said, "Freddy's troops are dumb; next time they should try wearing advanced eyeglasses so they can see in the dark."

They came out to empty city streets, clean places without garbage that looked very well maintained. There were entertainment buildings everywhere, from theaters to dance — the site was terrific.

Gustave was fascinated and said, "Look, sir, even though it is not as beautiful as my old New Paris, this city reminds me how beautiful the planet used to be."

"Don't worry, Colonel," Marco said, "I am sad because Wonderland chose to fight us. We will get revenge for all the destruction Dragon has done one day!"

Gustave and Marco then ran into an empty cafe. Gustave said, "Sir, it's a pity that we must destroy this place because its leaders won't let us go."

They entered and sat on the second floor. Gustave asked, "What are we doing here, sir? This shop is closed."

"No," Marco replied. "We're hiding until help arrives — I've done this a lot."

After sitting for a while, a hologram of Constantine appeared in their midst.

Marco was shocked and asked, "How can you appear here?!" Constantine said, "Gentlemen, I am a god in Wonderland. My replican brain is directly connected to all systems in the city of

Wonderland—I don't have a physical body, only a Cyber body. You can't hide from the god of Wonderland!"

Marco said to him, "Let us go, and no one will get hurt or die."

Constantine responded, "No, Gent, you do not understand; the replica in Wonderland is the future of the planet. We are aware that we are new humans. Even though we have old memories, we are still new creations. If you bring an old war going on between humans and dragons, then you will only bring death. Stop it before it's too late."

"NO!" Marco roared. "I will not die here. I will get out of here. You have all slept for quite a while without doing anything about the killer of this place; those dragons are laughing at your pathetic life."

The hologram then became unstable. "There is something wrong, sir!" Gustave said to Marco.

Then Gustave pulled Marco out of the seat and jumped from the cafe, not long after, Constantine's hologram blew himself up with a plan to kill Marco but failed; apparently the hologram of Constantine was carried by a small bomb drone that flew. The explosion brought city patrols, and many troops came to Marco and Gustave.

Both of them then headed away from the building and found an amusement park filled with carnivals, but the place was empty. The festival was close to the border wall and port. They found a bus that resembled an electric train—the bus used for tourist purposes. Marco and Gustave took the vehicle down a road that swooped down. It seemed that it went straight down the hill of the city.

"Look, sir, we are in the small Francisco sector, I think," Gustave said.

Gustave drove the bus down the steep hill; buildings with decorated lights and candles were everywhere. While they rode the bus, a crowd of people and robots appeared on the road going berserk. The people came screaming in various languages mixed from all over European, which confused Marco. They then stoned Marco with bricks and stones.

"Sir!" Gustave asked, "How is this?"

"They are just replicas and brainwashed robots; they want to kill us —just pass," Marco answered in a rush.

"Well, sir, I will pass as if they were just statues," Gustave said.

Then Gustave drove the bus down without looking at the road —at the bridge Gustave crashing into the crowd of robots.

Marco rebuked Gustave, saying, "Colonel, are you crazy? We will be seen as bad guys by these people."

Gustave said, "Sir, welcome to our planet. Where you have to take a hit or beat each other."

Some Replicas tried to stop them with carts and cars, but Gustave buss-trains are large enough to destroy all barricades. The bus continues to go down to the end of the hill like a running deer, where there is a gate to enter the amusement park. The gate could also be crashed, so they came to the nearest Constantine statue, where their sturdy bus was destroyed when it hit the figure. That forced Marco out with Gustave. They had to go forward into the amusement park to get to the nearest port where Gustave's troops were fighting.

"Come on, sir," Gustave said. "Don't look back; the sea is the most feared by robots. We can be safe there."

After a little trouble with the bus door, Gustave and Marco finally got out. A crowd of people —from Replicas to ordinary civil robots —came towards Marco angrily. They were carrying weapons such as assemblies, wooden spears, and axes and were the militia of civilians who were initiated by Constantine to protect the city. The crowd was still well-dressed, wearing suits, fancy cloth pants, ties, hats, and even flowers that were tacked on the clothes. With a metal plate and small armor, the Militia advanced without fear. A struggle to save the imaginary world created by Replicas from Wonderland; feeling comfortable with their position, they will not just give up, but let their dreams for a moment disappear in the fire of war by fighting.

Marco was shocked to see the crowds from the city heading toward him. Frightened, he said, "Colonel, try making a fire fence; don't let the crowd approach."

"Good, sir." Gustave answered, spitting out the remaining heat on the tube and spraying it like a wall of fire.

Marco then flew up, but the pilot's shirt was slightly damaged so he could not fly high.

"Don't get too high, sir!" Gustave said, "They can shoot you easily if they are in the sky."

The wall of fire managed to stop the Militias, so only Marco and Gustave were left. They then went to the port through the amusement park. The place looked like it was a festival, with lots of balloons and food scattered everywhere.

Marco became suspicious and said, "Colonel, this place looks too quiet, very suspicious for a densely populated city. Something is wrong."

Constantine's hologram again appeared in the middle of a field at the festival. Constantine said, "All of The Seven stars from the north are: North Star Union, House of Reich, The Raymond Palace, Radford Factorium, United Kingdom of Lavish, The Great Republic of Grandeville, and Mega Electra 20! The remnants of all of us have been united for a hundred years building the great city of Wonderland; we will not let you destroy this!"

Marco and Gustave continued to move forward in spite of Constantine's warning. Constantine said again, "I will not let you go; even the whole city and I will do everything we can to maintain peace!" The voice of Constantine was so loud that it made the place tremble.

From behind the hologram of Constantine, there were many

more militias; this time, they were festival people who dressed like many mascots and wore different clothes. Militia from the festival ran after Marco and Gustave. Some Militia did acrobatic movements, some used unique tools that make them fly, and others chased with decorative cars and even a single-wheeled bicycle. Joy can turn into evil; worse, both occur together. Produce something that looks silly to them, but his heart has no mercy or guilt.

"Oh, no, sir." Gustave said to Marco. "Look, they're militia and try to chase us with the festival clown."

Marco flew up to the roof of a low-rise amusement park but was chased by strange robots who used propellers like helicopters. Some were wearing balloons, and some were using propeller planes carrying lots of colored smoke. Marco tried to avoid the pursuit of the people by twirling and circling back. A festival helicopter-propeller approached, and Marco shot him until the propeller hit the balloon near him, which fell over and closed the pilot's face on the propeller plane until they all fell from a single shot.

"Good shot, sir." Gustave said, looking down from the radio.

"Not safe on the roof," Marco said, and then jumped down again.

Some clowns with homemade weapons chased them too. Marco hit one of them and destroyed the body of that robot.

"Look at that, colonel," Marco said. "I can't recognize between Replicas and ordinary robots. They are all crazy."

Gustave stepped closer to Marco and said, "Look there, sir; the special forces of Santa Constantine are approaching."

"Freddy?" Marco reacted fearfully.

Then came many robots wearing Santa Claus costumes.

"Colonel, let's find a way out," Marco said in a somewhat angry tone.

While the festival robots were gathered, there were several

replicas of thick-armor-wearing, robust Mecha robots with large spears. Gustave's heat power was exhausted so he could no longer make fire, so Marco and he sprinted out of the crowd of robots. Freddy's knights, who wore Mecha, advances. Regardless of the reed, the Mecha crashed and even cut to pieces the festival robots that stood in their way.

The Replica Knights shouted, using speakers, "Get out of the way; let the Hjalmar Fredsbevarer knights pass by. FOR SANTO CONSTANTINE OUR LORD ANSGAR!"

Meanwhile, in the harbor, Gustave's army was fully occupied, even though their commander was trapped with Marco in the city. The robotic forces continued to advance, installing many assembled mortars and catapults to shoot the city wall. The beautiful city of Wonderland was layered with five rows of giant yellow walls, and in the middle was the largest palace on the planet—the residence of Saint Constantine which was heavily guarded by Fredsbevarer or Freddy. Marco saw Gustave's forces move forward even without regard to them.

"Why are your troops advancing?" Marco asked.

Gustave replied, "Don't worry, sir. To put things together, first, you must destroy the separating wall."

Worried, Marco asked, "Are you going to destroy this city, colonel? This city is too strong."

Alexa also called Gustave. "Good idea, colonel, but first, get Marco out of the trap. I have started successfully inviting STARS forces to attack the city, and some STARS troops have begun to take my bait towards the border."

"How did you do this? STARS aren't that stupid, or are they foolish?" Marco asked Alexa, who could also hear his call.

Alexa replied, "All STARS robots are controlled by one passionate and crazy AI. STARS will be stunned to see this big rich city; of course, they will be very savage looking for resources there."

CHAPTER 11

Marco and Gustave continued to go towards the harbor, gradually getting closer, while Freddy's troops were still trapped inside the festival crowd. But there was one giant yellow wall that they had to pass before entering the city in the port, and the wall was one hundred meters tall. Then there was a large mill around it; the amusement wheel was spinning while it was attached to the giant wall. Marco and Gustave went looking for the entrance to get out of the last wall. A gate is wide open there and looked unguarded.

Feeling suspicious, Marco did not dare to advance. He saw a row of palm trees along the road, indicating that the port was near.

"Sir, it looks like we have to find another way," Gustave said, stopping Marco.

He said, "Yes Colonel, the wide open gate is too suspicious. What should we do?"

"Let's wait—we'll see what will happen," Gustave answered, as they went to the nearest building to look for another way.

A large building—a magnificent and spacious museum—was found on the edge of a quiet street. Glancing behind them, they saw Freddy's troops approaching with robotic horses.

Pointing to the building, Gustave said, "Sir, let's go protect ourselves in the building."

The two walked through the large door of the museum building. Once inside, they found a large and empty hall. Marco tried to go further because he was curious about the museum.

Marco asked Gustave, "Colonel, I wonder what this is. Isn't this supposed to be a museum? Why is it empty?"

Gustave answered, "A museum is an institution to preserve collections of artifacts and other objects that are important—artistic, cultural, historical, or scientific. Regarding why this place is empty, I don't know either."

Marco nodded his head. "Oh, it looks like the museum is empty because they purposely want to delete something out of history."

Suddenly a hologram appeared from Constantine—the first in a while. Constantine stood up and said, "Why are you trying to run away? I control this city. I am everywhere. I have eyes all over—give up, and I will spare your life. The promise of Saint Constantine will always be fulfilled. Praise my generosity, you wicked knekt."

"Stop it, old man. I will not grow old and die here without a fight," Marco angrily replied to Constantine.

Constantine said again: "I will offer you one more chance; understand that from the catastrophe, a new and better world was born. Just as on earth where the whole world of dinosaurs vanished instantly. Some said it was because the waves of meteors fell, and others claimed it was due to the floodwater. The same thing happened here because of plasma waves like a flood from the sky, but one thing we know—a new, better world arose from a devastating disaster. Follow me, forgive me, and I shall forgive you. Praise my generosity now."

"Do you worship Dragon? Don't you know that Dragon intends to destroy the entire planet with nothing left but dust?!" Marco snarled.

Hearing Marco's refusal, Constantine became disgusted and said, "No, not worshiping the dragon you fool. Enough! My mercy door is closed. You wicked knekt."

They were in the middle of the hall. Suddenly there appeared

Freddy's cavalry again—the cavalry jumping from the museum windows which were smashed to pieces like a boulder thrown on the glass. Many of Freddy's knights entered and surrounded them. Unable to go anywhere, Marco and Gustave were trapped in the hall. Silently, Freddy's forces surrounded them—but did not attack—and waited for the cue from Constantine.

"Look at the gentlemen; regret always comes late," Constantine said as he raised his hand.

Marco lifted his gun, pointing the barrel at Constantine. Seeing that, Colonel Gustave said, "Sir, what are you doing? He is just a hologram."

"I know," Marco answered, and then shot Constantine.

Marco's bullet strikes a bomb ball that usually flies close to the Constantine hologram—the ball of the drone used by Constantine as a speaker and bomb. The ball of the drone exploded, and the floor of the hall was destroyed. Everyone fell into the hole . . . the whole level cracked and collapsed into the underground. Marco fell into the underground—into a dark room and slammed to the floor there. He could see nothing because the place in the underground was very dark. Activating his night vision glasses, Marco was finally able to stand. After stepping his feet on sand, he looked around to find Gustave. The place did not have light; about fifty meters away from the base of the museum, there were many doorless aisles and stone walls. He could hear voices of Freddy's troops everywhere, communicating with each other to chase Marco. Being alone again, Marco tried to protect himself on the wall, but that made many skulls fall. Marco realized that the place was a catacomb, housing a mass grave underground. A large door opened from above, and many Freddy troops entered, filling from the top down to the bottom. The Museum turned out to be the entrance to the catacomb.

The tomb is a place to rest, but something eternal is not rest;

they do not sleep—only their creators have the power to wake the dead. A dark place that does not need light, like their hearts that are no longer glowing, sinking into a voiceless and unreal place in the underworld.

Realizing that, Marco thought, *Oh, the actual contents of the museum are in the underground. They keep it here so they can forget it.*

Marco looked for an escape from the catacomb. Freddy's troops continued to chase him from behind, searching for Marco in the dark. Marco continued to walk, searching everywhere. The wind was so cold, and a few small lights from a distance above the catacomb cave gave a little line of view. As he walked further, he saw bare roots that were blackened on the ground and some gray stone walls wrecked in the cave. The sound of Freddy's troops searching for him moved farther and farther away. Feeling safe, Marco tried to relax after being separated from the others. He was trying not to stumble; it felt like he was walking on sand but there were some things like bones that he stepped on. A Freddy warrior suddenly appeared with the Mecha he was wearing; the heavy Mecha had a long, thick steel sword. Freddy tried to slash Marco. Marco crashed against a large rock, and then tried to stand up but couldn't. Marco crawled slowly away because he was injured—the sword had slashed his stomach. Feeling that his opponent was helpless, Freddy then pounded Marco's head with the big butt of his sword. Marco's helm protected him, but his body fell hard on the ground. Fred's Mecha kicked Marco until he was thrown a few meters away. Feeling dizzy and sick, Marco tried to lift his gun. Marco Clarion's weapon was still tied to his shirt; seeing that, Freddy then proceeded to quickly step on Marco again— the beat of the robot's feet made the ground around him tremble, causing small rocks to fall.

As he approached, Freddy said, "For the sake of our Lord Constantine. Die you, mortal man!"

Marco dodged the large Mecha foot, which hit the ground

beneath it. Immediately, deep sand was brought down by the Mecha's feet, because, without knowing it, the Mecha was right at the edge of the cliff. Freddy and his Mecha fell with a landslide into the darkness. Marco felt strong again and stood up. As he searched, a vast dark chasm was visible in front of him; the cave was more extensive than he had thought from a distance, and there were damaged buildings in the dark cave. The place is not forgotten but hidden to not remember — the final place on the bottom, in the world of lifeless silence.

What is this place? He thought. *There is an old city in the underground of Wonderland. The place is full of bones and dead bodies like in New Paris on Grande.*

The fallen Mecha flashlight was still burning, about twenty meters deep in the ravine. Freddy, who was in Mecha, then shouted, "EVERYONE! That fresh flesh is here!"

Then Freddy shot a fire arrow from the crossbow up towards Marco. Marco quickly avoided the arrow, which accidentally hit another Mecha who was about to catch Marco from behind. The shot caused that Mecha to lose his direction. Marco immediately turned around and shot his head, but the black iron used by the Mecha Knights was almost impenetrable.

Mecha who was hit by the arrow shouted, "DAMN YOU, MORON! Hey, don't shoot friends like that; you suck."

The Mecha in the ravine answered, "Not my fault; I didn't see you before."

Marco quickly tried to avoid them, afraid that more Freddy troops were coming. He jumped towards the cliff and slid down the steep hillside. Without knowing where he was, Marco felt lost without Gustave.

Where is the big-head robot located? Marco thought, worried about his safety.

After arriving at the bottom, Marco saw a bright light in front of him.

This must be the way out, he thought.

Afraid of being trapped again, Marco continued walking forward, trying to stay out of sight. As he stepped forward, his feet began to get stuck in the bones in the cave. There were lots of skeletons—from animals to humans—there, many piled up to make dead hills. Trying to step lightly on his feet, Marco thought about the sad stories those bones represented; it saddened his heart at the thought of death. Step by step, Marco eased through the sea of skulls in that place. From above, a group of worker robots from the city of Wonderland was trying to dig up the site; they had made many holes so that light could enter. Electricity had not been connected for a long time in the cave, so troops of Wonderland used moonlight from space. Some flashlights were inserted from above, and the drones fluttered about with lights everywhere, all looking for Marco and Gustave. Walking a great distance, Marco went up and down the bone hills.

"Welcome to the Golgotha!" Constantine said from somewhere. "Welcome to our museum."

"That's him!" said a Freddy there.

Marco tried to run, but a Freddy came out of the pile of bones to catch Marco's feet.

"I caught him!" said the Freddy knight.

Marco kicked him, but he couldn't get free; then Marco shot him in the head, but a sturdy steel helmet protected his head. Finally, Marco's foot was freed. Wanting to run fast, the piles of bones were dense enough slow him. Some robots and Freddy appeared from inside the skull piles, shooting at Marco. Several bullets and bombs passed near enough to hurt him, but not too bad because they were using weak homemade weapons.

Marco shouted at them, "WHAT IS THIS? This is the grave of your ancestors of yourself; don't you have respect?!"

Constantine's voice was heard from the cave speaker somewhere, like an echo. "Don't you know, Mr. Marco? We are new people; do we have to cry for a hundred years? We are not part of them—we are a new creation, and thinking that we are human beings who have long been dead will not be useful. It will only bring death as you see here, like you who bring death to us."

Among those who have long fallen, become one with dust, as their lives are only dust among the stars. Marco ran between the hills of the skulls to protect himself; a pile of large elephant bones was there, and Marco took cover, hiding his body.

Annoyed, Marco raised his voice from the helm and replied "Don't forget who you are, and what bones are buried here. Pride and selfishness have blinded you with lust."

Constantine replied, "Then what is Mr. Marco? Revenge? You will lose. To survive? We have done it for one hundred years! This world is dead; don't make our world die, too. It's your selfishness, not mine."

More bullets explode around Marco, with bones flying everywhere. As he lowered his head, the Wonderland bullets pierced the skull hill inside the cave. Dead people in that place are just silent, they don't think, have no sense, because they are no longer there—just lost, vanished to hover among the underworld.

Marco shouted again at Constantine, saying, "DRAGON WILL RISE AGAIN, CONSTANTINE! When their strength has accumulated, there will be more plasma waves that not only kill all biology but also electricity—including any machine like you."

"You're lying!" Constantine said, "We have lived all this time peacefully. Dragon has lost his energy; if not, this is not the right time. You are too weak. Attacking Dragon Mount will only make them angry and they will destroy us again."

Several flying propellers carrying flashlights continued to find Marco's position, so he had to shoot them, but his places were increasingly visible. Marco had to be able to get out of the crowd.

A familiar voice was heard—it was Gustave standing on the

near stones. Gustave said, "Sir! Protect your head!"

That's what I'm doing, Marco thought.

Gustave then shot the city pipes connected underground which were above them, causing a lot of falling water to soak and flood the place. The large pipes made a strong wave of water and scattered many people away from the group. Marco tried to run up one of the skull hills to avoid the waves. The Wonderland robots began to get trapped, but some of Freddy's replicas managed to climb from the hills next to them, shooting at Marco; he shot back and hit one of them. The bullets sparked on Freddy's armor. Freddy was not injured but fell down and rolled into the water. Because of the weight of their armor, some Freddie's sank and could not swim. The water also damaged some of them. They were a century-old Android human robots that were often repaired; that electrical short circuit kills them if they are too long under water.

Constantine saw that and became angry. "Attack that man! I don't care if I have to lose hundreds of knights—make that human virus disappear so that it doesn't spread the disease. We will lose hundreds of Replicas today so thousands of other Replicas will live."

Many Freddy knights tried to climb up the bone hills to shoot Marco who was also trapped. An explosion occurred when one of Freddy's threw a homemade grenade, causing Marco to fall into the water.

Then Gustave said on the radio, "Sir, take it easy; your clothes are waterproof."

Marco replied, "Hey Colonel, why haven't we been talking on the radio? How ridiculous we are. I will swim towards you."

Marco swam like a torpedo in the water, thanks to the help of his pilot's clothes, and reached Gustave's position without being detected.

Gustave said, "Come on, sir! I have found the net leading us out; let's go here."

The two then rushed out of the vast and dark Catacomb's cave. Without any more interference from Constantine's troops, they managed to get out past a long, industrial ladder. Left and right of them there were skull walls—also multiple holes with deep, dark bottoms. The place was filled with countless corpses and skulls, as large as the city of Wonderland. The staircase was so long; far up, slowly the light began to shine brightly and warmed Marco's body. He felt like someone had just risen from the grave; his body was battered and covered in wounds. Leaving a buried place, something beautiful above, nicely decorated, but inside is just a bone . . . that's the city of Wonderland. It's like a tomb decorated, but it has fading contents, just like its inhabitants.

After reaching the end of the stairs, Gustave said, "Sir! Congratulations, we have arrived outside."

* * *

The two of them walked out through a crypt. Marco looked back and saw a large golden yellow wall—they had made it through the wall from under the ground. Several large-headed soldiers of the Gustave robots were waiting for them outside.

One of the robots said, "Colonel, only we have made it; most of the troops are still trapped in the port, far from here."

Marco saw Gustave and said proudly, "Colonel Gustave, your troops are very talented for the size of an ordinary robot that is not android. I am very impressed."

"Thank you, sir. I'm also curious; how did you know that there was a cave behind the museum floor?" Gustave asked.

Marco replied "When we walked in, the floor did not sound solid, when Constantine's hologram appeared, I caused his drone to explode and open the way if possible. That managed to make us fall into the catacomb and separated us from the trap of Constantine. We could have just died or tried anything that we could."

"Sir, let's continue the journey. I believe the enemy is watching us," Gustave said as he drove his group out along a path.

The city streets were made of bricks, and the walls of the city buildings were like gold, with lots of colorful flags, decorative lights, balloons, and other decorations along the way. Plastic flowers and trees were planted in various places, the beautiful Wonderland city amazed Marco and brought a moment of peace to his heart. The city streets were hushed, but Gustave was careful.

"My army. We have to be careful; the Wonderland forces can be anywhere," Gustave said.

While guarding Marco and walking to the port, suddenly fifty Freddy troops showed up to trap them; also the hologram of Constantine appeared in the middle of their way.

"Again? What should we do now?" Marco said to his team in anger.

Constantine's hologram stood up and said, "Enough! Gentlemen, that's enough! Bow now and kneel before me, let me shoot you in a way that isn't painful."

"WE WILL NOT, YOU SANTA CLAUS!" Gustave shouted with his robotic voice. "Even though you see my troops as ordinary wreckage robots, I will prove that our enthusiasm is enough to destroy even a powerful and smart Android robot technology like Replica."

"Doesn't anyone have manners any more? As you wish," Constantine said before ordering Freddy's troops to shoot them.

CHAPTER 12

Gustave and his small army began to take up arms while aiming at the face of Freddy's knight. Marco looked around, searching for another way out but he could not see one.

"It's over! I'm here; thank you, Gustave. Forgive me, friends. Sorry, Monica, for not being able to save you. I will fail here," Marco said, as he stood looking at Constantine.

All hope was exhausted. The two sides exchanged glances at one another. Sweat began to cover him, and Marco's heartbeat became strong. Everyone was waiting to see who would take the first shot. Suddenly something happened, stopping the tense situation; an abundant light emerged from above the sky — bright light like fire descended slowly towards the base of the planet where they stood. The meteor was large enough to pass through the Phoenix energy shield that was in the atmosphere and enter without being heavily damaged.

A Freddy shouted in fear, "DRAGON ATTACK! THEY WILL DESTROY US!"

Constantine said, "No, gentlemen, it is a meteor. Sadly, I think the meteor is big enough to destroy our city."

The meteor was seen falling right at the palace where Constantine's brain was — a golden palace in the middle of the golden walls that surrounded it.

With sad eyes, Constantine looked at Marco, "Mr. Marco, I really hate you but remember if you want to kill Dragon and take our revenge, meet my granddaughter named Nora; she will help you. Good luck, you wicked knekt."

They did not know what happened because the place where the meteor fell was hidden by a high, golden wall; the meteorite fell right at Constantine's palace, and it made the hologram of Constantine disappear immediately — Constantine had vanished completely. Meteor clashes on the ground made everyone shake and fall to the ground; most of the buildings collapsed due to the impact. A massive wave of fire erupted from where the meteor fell, but the stream of fire dust was blocked by five large wall circles around the palace of Constantine. But the wave still rose, destroying the walls and burning down each side of the place. Gustave robots' legs were broken, but somehow Marco and Gustave survived. After the quake, shockwaves destroyed many objects, along with the city. Things right behind the bottom of the wall that was not destroyed were protected from the strong winds. Some walls cracked and pieces fell on several people below. When it was over, Marco and Gustave continued their journey to the port.

Marco was stunned. "A meteor that falls in the middle of the city? That is impossible; it must have been planned; is this a tactic from UW or Central?"

Both of them ran, dodging flames and chunks of the wall that were falling.

Gustave replied, "Sir, whatever it is, it saved us. It must have come from your friends from outer space."

"So, so far we are being observed? We are just an experiment for them; brash," Marco said irritably.

"Or, we are the only remaining remnant. You are the second human who made it to the surface of the planet after Lee was killed ten years ago," said Gustave.

Some collapsed wall bricks the size of a large building almost fell on Marco. While thick smoke from cement debris began to rise, it filled the environment and obstructed their vision.

"THAT'S THEM, THOSE BASTARDS!" shouted someone

hidden in the smoke.

"Yes!" said another person. "Those who made our beloved Saint Constantine die."

The brain from the hologram of Constantine came from that palace when it was destroyed by a meteor; he vanished, angering his followers. Freddy's highest-ranking general began to take control; he was named Arthur Løve who was nicknamed Boneheart because of his discipline, and he vowed to kill Marco. He would bring big trouble later. Marco and Gustave walked among the ruins of the city. Fire and smoke were everywhere. They walked while hiding themselves among the chaos caused by the meteor.

Gustave said, after seeing it, "Look, sir! Plastic palm trees begin to appear; the port where my troops are is near."

Some of the remaining Wonderland robotic troops came out trying to shoot them. There were also some Freddy robots who came out looking for them. Between the fire and the city that burned, Marco walked between the halls filled with disaster. After a while, a light emerged from the thickness of the smoke; an armored assembled vehicle from Gustave's forces seemed to be approaching through the dense dust, and hope came back to them.

"It's close; we'll get out of here," Gustave said, carrying Marco by holding it.

Unbeknownst to them, a rocket fell in the middle of them, the missile exploded, and an EMP wave came out that killed many robots around it, Gustave was also hit but survived by falling a little. Then, from above, came a tall robot with big hands, catching Marco with one hand and then inserting him into his stomach. The giant robot was wearing a large gas cylinder on his back. After retrieving Marco, the robot jumped again very high to take him away. The robot had two legs like the one that used boost power that could make it jump high, thanks to the power of the gas that was stored in it.

The operator who controlled the Mecha said, "Yeah! Ha ha ha ha! My name is Stefan von Cortlandt, but you can call me Dutchman! I will take you to lady. I hope you don't move too much, let me be the one who moves too much."

The operator named Dutchman was wearing expensive clothes, a sailor captain's hat, and a tie in the glass of the steam robot. He was an Android Replica, and he took Marco up to the buildings with his Mecha.

Nervous, Marco said, "Take me out! What else is this? I am not interested in it."

Dutchman doesn't care and said, "Yes, but no! Sorry, I just carry out the orders!"

Alexa immediately connected with Gustave, and then sent Gustave airplanes to chase him. The thick smoke and fire made it difficult for pilots to find a Dutchman who kept jumping up and down like a frog among the ruined buildings of the Wonderland city. Some of the lands were split due to the earthquake and opened up the catacomb to make the buildings sink into the underground. Dutchman almost fell with his robot, but he nimbly managed to avoid many new ravines. A pilot saw the Dutchman, and then flew to chase and shoot him but missed. Dutchman then entered into a large building where the train station was while he continued to run and jump. He met with Fred's troops who were inside.

One Freddy said, "Hey, Dutchman, stop it! Where are you going?"

Dutchman ignored them and kept moving. The windows of the train station were large, so several of Gustave's aircraft crashed through and found them. There were engagement between Freddy and Gustave's army plane. Dutchman kept jumping up and down while destroying many objects in front of him. Marco, who was in the stomach of the Dutchman robot, became dizzy even though there were many pillows inside. Because the station building was filled with lots of poles, many Gustave planes were destroyed by crashing into them. Because it flew low, there was even a Freddy who managed to jump cut one of the aircraft with his knight Mecha.

* * *

After all the battles inside the train station, Dutchman managed to get out of the building and arrived at the large city park. Falling meteors had destroyed many of the Wonderland's defenses, and many of their aircraft still at the airport were also destroyed. The unstable land due to the earthquake from the fall of the meteor created a giant crevice between the city of Wonderland and Catacomb city below. There were many of Freddy's soldiers, much artillery, and anti-air weapons that continued to shoot the sky outside. Smoke, fire, ash, and the ruins of large buildings flew everywhere. While landslides still occurred and made many parts of the city sink into the ground, Catacomb's cave was large. Gustave's reconnaissance fighters and Zeppelins began to appear in the air, leaving the remaining Wonderland troops overwhelmed. Dutchman then jumped into the middle of the battlefield; while he ran, he continued to be chased by the pilot. A Zeppelin threw a massive bomb which fell and exploded almost on Dutchman; the blast made a large hole that led to the collapsing of road into the ground.

Alexa said, "Colonel Gustave! Command the troops to be careful; disable the robot but be careful, because your shots can kill Marco, our hero."

"All right, my lady, I'll try," Gustave answered.

The Gustave's propeller began flying and tried to trap the Dutchman by shooting his feet using a machine gun. But the destruction they made helped make the city collapse into the ground. Hundreds of thousands of replicas from Wonderland came out against Gustave's troops, but Alexa had brought in more Gustave robots from Grande; the robots were mostly civil robots modified into combat engines, like their vehicles. Because of the quake caused by the meteor, many Wonderland soldiers who participated were buried in landslides, fallen into Catacomb caves located in the lower part of the city. The Dutchman managed to avoid all of that and continued to jump like an agile frog.

Gustave asked Alexa who continuously watched from the satellite above the city, "Mrs. Alexa, where do you think the robot took Marco? Because it seems to have something to do with Constantine's granddaughter named Nora."

"Nora?" asked Alexa, "I have never heard of her before, but from the direction of his movement, it seems that the Mecha tried to take Marco to a big villa far away."

After escaping, Dutchman said to Marco, "Hey, hey, sir! Sorry, we will start walking more calmly now."

The Dutchman stopped running and walked through many sheltered places to avoid being seen from skywatchers of Gustave's army aircraft.

"Where are they, my lady? The grasshopper has managed to get rid of its tracks!" Gustave said with an annoying robotic voice, mocking the Dutchman robot.

Alexa said, "He started hiding, best to keep watching by land."

There were underground railways, so the Dutchman freely walks past unnoticed, and then heads to a villa in the middle of a large plastic green lawn garden near the Wonderland border. Arriving there, he took Marco right to the door of the large villa. The red moonlight illuminated the lawn, and it looked like it was daytime even though the sky was visible at night. A large distress antenna at Dutchman Mecha was damaged and blocking the radio's signal connection between Marco and his friends, leaving him isolated from the others.

Feeling sick and dizzy, Marco tried to stand up. He saw the vast meadow and said "What else is this place? Football field?"

Dutchman, while standing near Marco, said, "Yes sir! I use it to play and jump here. But lady doesn't like it; she's happy to let this place go to waste and unused. Awful!"

"Oh, I think you want me to go into that big villa, don't you?" Marco asked.

Dutchman submitted to his robot and made a move. "Please, sir!"

Marco then walked along, following him for fear that he would be forced again' he walked towards the streets carved out of stone, through the short, plastic grass, and then up the stairs of the grand white villa. Arriving inside, the villa looked empty but was immaculately clean. The place was far from where the meteor fell, so it was still intact. Five massive golden walls blocked the meteor shockwave. Beautiful place near the sea, at the end of the city, there are many relaxing places and plastic palm trees, but quite far from the harbor.

The Dutchman then followed Marco with his Mecha, showing the way while saying, "Go up the stairs, sir! Please do not be shy; make yourself at home."

With worried smile, Marco climbed the broad staircase; on the left and right were many plastic flowers, paintings, classic music instrument, and old books. After walking through several rooms, Marco arrived at a room filled with a collection of colored bottles; there was calm and sad viola music from a loudspeaker. Suddenly, things look different, like in another world, not like in outside where death and war still happened.

"What place is this?" He asked the Dutchman.

Dutchman answered, "Lady Nora's workroom."

He went on. Further in, he saw many statues standing there. Curious, Marco touched an old Musketeer statue and found that the figure was just a plastic mold, a strong one.

"Welcome to my villa; don't get me wrong, but I'm more happy in my cabin than this place where my grandpa forced me to stay. Tell me, do you like my Redcoat version of the Nutcracker?" asked a woman a short distance away.

Marco was shocked and looked forward—there was a replica in the form of a small child, with white hair, and she was holding and looking at a little bird-shaped toy in her hand.

"She is Lady Nora Ylva," Dutchman said, whispering to Marco.

Nora then looked at Marco. He saw that the little woman was dressed neatly in a white leather jacket and black tie.

"Let me guess," Marco calmly said. "You will beat me up. But I didn't kill your grandfather. I feel sorry, too, but I did not send the meteor. It was them, the Central."

"You didn't answer my question," Nora said.

"Sorry again, little kid. Yes, I like your Redcoat plastic sculpture," he answered.

Suddenly, suddenly Nora roared, "I AM NOT A KID; I AM A HUNDRED AND THIRTEEN YEARS OLD! Then she pelted Marco with a bird toy from her hand. Marco quickly lowered his head to make it miss.

Nora chuckled to see Marco falling to the floor.

Nora advanced and stood in front of Marco. "Do you feel lonely, Mr. Marco?"

"This place is too crowded, so I'm not" Marco answered.

Nora said, "I have a friend; we have always played together since childhood, and he is a small young man. But when plasma waves almost hit our country, we were all forced to sleep. When we woke up, it turned out we were just robots, and our old selves were dead to dust. I am not Nora—I am just an AI with the memory of her, the little girl."

Confused, Marco asked, "So? What's the connection with me?"

Dutchman then hit Marco's head with the hand of the Mecha robot he was wearing. Marco fell back to the floor, and Dutchman said, "Don't cut people off; it's rude."

Marco was angry and thought, *That's strange, when beating people's heads is being polite.*

Nora continued, "I woke up a few years later with an android body as a Replica. I only dreamed that I would be able to play with my family and the boy, forever in a large lawn garden full of trees with fragrant flowers. But none of them woke up; the plasma wave killed several of the sleeping Replicas. And I only met my grandfather, Ansgar, whom you called Constantine. Unfortunately, he changed, and forced his will that a Replica must live a new life without connecting with life from his memory. I always hated that, but it's useful. He's the prick who also started the world war a long time ago, so I've hates him since the beginning and always. Too bad he died, too. Somehow I didn't feel really sorry—it's strange. Perhaps because I'm lack of biologic hormones. I know this feeling exists, but it's too confusing to explain."

Marco tried to stand again. From the look on his face, it was clear that he was bored. Dutchman then grabbed Marco's head and forced him to look at Nora.

Nora said again, "You too dear, you must forget your old life. Be a Replica."

Marco released his head from the grip of the Dutchman robot, walked backward, and said, "Become a Replica? I know it's not the process of moving memory but copying it to AI; that process will kill me. You're killing my soul."

"Listen, dear," Nora said with a silly seductive tone. "I know you will reject it; I'm just joking, even though I want it. I will help you fight the Dragon."

Marco taunted her. "It's strange to hear those words coming out of the mouth of a child, even though she's a robot. No, thanks, I already have friends."

Nora then chuckled again, she said "Friends? They tricked you; they are agents of Central robots from Cyber Autocrazy. Have you ever asked how Alexa could be the only survivor when Dragon attacked the entire Replica in Grande ten years ago, because they protected a human named Lee? Or how could there be a civilian robot with a brain as super intelligent as Gustave?"

Marco was surprised. "Wait, how? No one can enter or exit the planet."

"You can't trust them," Nora said.

With scorned face, Marco said "Oh, like somehow I can trust you, stranger."

Nora replied, "They think we are stupid — maybe Replica in a stupid Wonderland. But not me, after observing from a distance. They are not from out there, but from Central countries on this planet called Mega Electra 20, the Central Research State. It might be the only place that can communicate with the outside world secretly, signaling that they managed to get through the Phoenix cage in the atmosphere. But as you can see, here, we're always busy with festivals and parties."

"Why are you always busy with a lot of festivals and art in this place?" Marco asked.

Nora answered, "Festival and art? It is the way we remember the past and remember those who have died. This place was very popular with arts, even other colonies imitated us, like the colonies of Nova Anglia who began to sculpting on their boring buildings. We used to had a huge influence."

Marco said with spirit, "Do you know? Thousands of years ago there were often the same festivals for my descendants; the festival was called the Día de los Muertos, or Day of the Dead — to commemorate those who have died."

"Interesting," said Nora, "I've read about it. There is a lot of literature in here and I have enough time to read. I like your way."

"All right, little girl, quite politely, tell me what your plan is? I mean, what do you want me to do?" Marco asked, although he was still hesitant.

CHAPTER 13

Nora took a small stick in her right hand, and then gave Marco her left hand. Spontaneously, Marco gave her his right hand and she held it while guiding him to another room. Dutchman continued to guard from behind and followed them observing that Marco remained scared. They passed down a dark staircase and through a room full of cover cloths along the door. There was a solid wall built with advanced metal technology, so the building there was not cracked due to the meteor. They arrived at a control room where there was a large screen. Marco just stood motionless. Nora then pulled him to a lever there.

Marco was confused and asked, "What is this?"

Nora replied, "We will get revenge on the people who killed your true friends. Central. This button will release my secret nuclear weapon towards the Mega Electra 20 state in the northeast. The Dragon can become stronger with a nuclear blast so no. Second, you go to the south and meet Prince Mikhail or Michael but don't kill him."

"Not so fast," Marco said. He remained suspicious. "I still don't believe you, and we just met. By the way, who the hell is this prince?"

Angry, Nora hit Marco with the stick she held on her head, which made Marco feel dizzy for a moment. Nora then said, "Who gives you a choice? Mr. Marco, you are just an experiment; by attacking Dragon, it will only make the old incident happen again. This planet has been sold by UW to Central. Destroy their plan; make them go down by themselves. The meteor was made by Central in space; they started playing dirty. We must destroy the Central."

Marco became confused, making him even more upset. He raised his hand. "Wait, wait! Let me think!"

Nora said, "There isn't enough time to think for you. I've done it for a long time. Come with me. I've been dead for a long time, destroying the Dragon is impossible. You have to join me to destroy the Central first. All your friends are dead; forget them. You have no choice—those robots are not your true friends. You have been tricked since the beginning; you and all your true friends died for nothing. Stop following their game."

Seeing that they were still fighting, Dutchman said, "My lady, stop. The time is running the same as the approaching enemy."

Feeling dizzy and confused, Marco's became disoriented. He froze up and just stood like a statue in a tricky situation. Instantly, like an arrow piercing in the chest, what had been held for a long time appeared on the surface, a struggle to forget the sad event, mixed with feelings of anger at feeling cheated, lost, and approaching death.

Then he remembered his friends and thought, *Monica, Franky, and others. They really are dead, I'm just trying to forget about all this mess. What should I do? Why am I the only one who has a soul? This is not fair."*

He always wants to be angry, but always to himself; now, he sees another object of anger, that is to people who are likely to have deceived him all this time.

Anger mixed with sadness because Nora pierced his heart. Marco started to leave but Dutchman tried to stop him. Nora chuckled. Marco entered a large room with a high dome; there were many statues and paintings from a century before. Marco began to realize, buried feelings were not good to keep in a long time; he had to get them out, so he could be relieved, but not to be swallowed up by them—he still has to be careful.

"Art? Fine work? What's the use for the lifeless! I'm sorry, not because I hate this, I must do this—release my anger that I have held all this time," Marco said, shouting and then attacking the room. He pelted paintings here and there and kicked carved statues. Many items were destroyed, the figures were broken, and the frames of the pictures were snapped.

Marco shouted as he continued to destroy the place, the sound of anger and sadness echoing in the dome. He was devastated because all his misery was only a game for others. A human who loses hope for his desires will be brought too many trials because of his own hard heart. Because it is true—that problems only exist if we believe they exist—the problem we are trying to hide is like oil and can be burned by other people or our emotions. But that behavior all comes from the desires of our own heart, the desire to destroy or build.

"Who says I don't like art?" Nora said, holding and playing her violin as she liked, the melody clear to Marco. Nora then walked while dancing towards the man. The fast tune was dance style but it suggested horror. Nora continued to play it.

After destroying many things, Marco's anger subsided as he finally listened to the music. Marco said, "It's useless; it's useless to shoot lifeless people. Just like you, Central is just a robot."

Nora began to play the violin with a slow tempo and said "Nothing is useless; all actions will get results, the bigger it is, the greater the results even for lifeless things—like a nuke. Tell me, handsome, how long will you continue to waste your valuable time?"

"Señorita, how much time do I have?" Marco asked.

Nora replied with a small laugh, she said, "No, my caballero . . . I'm just joking. You are just a walking corpse who waits for time to lose his life and whenever that can happen, without having to wait."

"Your words blur, but it still makes sense," Marco said with a limp face.

All of his struggles to survive and all of his friends who die are like games for others. Marco took off his gloves and looked at his palms, feeling sorry for himself. Nora took hold of Marco's bloody hand. Her hand felt very cold, like metal, and Marco's hand looked red as he drained blood.

Nora said, "Beautiful hands, beautiful art, a good creation. Tell me Marco, who is your Creator? Because it seems like as a robot, I have two. I always jealous of living people."

He then sat on the floor between the dirty stuff and asked Nora, who still played her violin calmly, "Tell me, little lady, do you still have dreams? Can Android really make its own dreams from previous memory?"

Looking at Marco with a sharp look, from her white robotic eyes, Nora answered, "I'm not sure; a dream is useless for robots. Why should they do it? But if the desire to realize your desire is a dream, then yes, I have a dream, because your dreams are now my dream. Take it, use this mirror every time you are angry; your anger will stop—not sure for you, but it worked for me."

While holding the small mirror and putting it in his shirt, Marco said, "Am I chosen? Why do I live, does Dragon let me live?" Marco asked.

Nora said as she continued to play the violin, "There is a story, a century ago according to the date of the earth, or fifty years ago according to the annual date of the Apen planet. The power of Dragon was brought by people, there's a royal people from the south who is also the most powerful ruler in their country, they wanted to use that power to bring peace and make themselves superhero. With Central, they got it after an expedition in the Carina Dwarf galaxy that was not so far from the Milky Way."

"Dragon is now a threat to other colonies world," Marco said. "The Felidean called it the Corrupted Seraphim. The power of fire stayed in the stars as its home and was about to destroy all the colonies in the galaxy."

Nora also said, "People was promised the power of a small star, almost an infinite power to defeat anything in the galaxy. But according to the legend, with that dangerous power, everyone wanted to attack the south and destroy their country in the south out of fear. The story was almost the same when humans attacked Neo-humans on Antarctica for fear of being replaced by super biological humans. Suddenly Dragon Wave happened because it invited the Dragon itself, and only a prince from the royal family who's still alive. Somehow."

"Maybe he wants to meet me. It's ridiculous; he might have been killed by a dragon," Marco said, not believing in his own statement.

Nora then suddenly hit Marco with her violin bow, which startled him. Nora said, "Get up! What's your dream?"

Marco stood up straight from his seat and said with enthusiasm, "Beat the Dragon so I can get out from this cemetery planet."

"No, you're dumb; you can't beat the Dragon, even with the entire army of this planet. You must find the Prince; I believe he's still alive because he's mighty, somehow," said Nora "Stay away from Central; they have tricked your group into coming here and they can still cheat you later."

"What's the plan?" Marco asked, confused.

"Go south, convince the replicas that are still sleeping there, and then attack the southern mountain with perfect tactics without interfering, because Central wants that technology. Unlike northern countries, Replicas in southern countries are still asleep for a century. Get out of here, Wonderland can't be changed; life is too long to make Replicas here become self-love. If you enter successfully, look for the prince. If he's dead or not there, then you die. Don't worry; I will look for your brain and make you my husband."

"That plan was silly. Why don't you go yourself?" He asked.

Nora answered, "Because you're the only human! The only one with a dream; your dreams are mine now. Everyone here is a dead person—they will listen to you. Go there, while I destroy the Central from here."

Marco wanted to walk but didn't know which way to go. He asked again, "Which door should I go to? Then what about your nuclear?"

Nora replied, "Dutchman, my loyal servant will take you to my private jet named Thor. While nuclear, let me shoot it; your dream now is my dream."

* * *

The Dutchman then came out, this time without Mechanic, and said, "Come here, sir! Remove your radio, don't get tracked! Come with me, it's time to fly south."

While they were still inside, from outside the magnificent villa, Freddy's troops began to arrive to find Marco and to arrest him. This made Alexa suspicious, so he also sent Gustave's forces there. There was a fierce battle that burned Nora's lawn garden, and it made Nora angry. Nora looked through her big windows, and saw that the garden had been damaged by a bomb, the trees were on fire, and the flowers were also burned. The replica plastic garden was melted by fire, and, with the stench reaching her nose, she felt that her yard had been charred before her eyes.

Nora said to herself as she walked back down the stairs "No!

No more—don't be burned by sadness; it's too painful to cry without tears!"

The garden she had built to memorialize her old life was destroyed. Angry, Nora quickly went to the control room to fire a nuclear towards the country of Mega Electra, the place of Central's secret command center.

While walking towards the runway, Marco and Dutchman increasingly dropped down instead of going up. It turned out that their track was under water.

Marco hesitated but thought, *I don't know, is Alexa really not Central or Nora who has a stupid assumption. But I have to get out of here, not to be influenced by anger again.*

An underwater tunnel, formed with glass around it, extends to the middle of the ocean. There is a different aircraft base, used so that the enemy cannot be detected in the air.

"Where are we going, Dutchman?" Marco asked when they got on their plane.

Dutchman replied, "Just calm down, sir! Uh, we're going to a faraway place in the southern country!"

Both of them then flew an aircraft named Thor, far beyond the ocean without anyone knowing. Gustave warships that were on the water did not know that. Marco saw two torpedoes from under the sea gliding; the projectile then began to fly up, past their Thor planes from out of the sea.

"What is that?" Marco asked in wonder.

Dutchman replied, "That! That's Lady Nora's nuclear!"

It was a surprise. Marco responded, "What!? Where is the destination?"

Dutchman replied, "Yes, yes, according to Lady Nora, one for the Central country which is far away, and one for the STARS headquarters in Grande."

"But the STARS headquarters on Grande is right on the Alexa Tower; she will kill her!" Marco said.

"No, no," answered Dutchman. "Don't worry, Central robot must get your revenge!!"

Feeling helpless, Dutchman was also wearing a strong Mecha. Marco could only be silent without making a decision. Soon, the two nuclear hits Central's Mega Electra 20 state and STARS headquarters in Grande. That makes a lot of robots from Gustave's forces experience signal interference, many of the planes falling down by themselves. The destroyed STARS headquarters made them angry, so many aircraft and the remaining STARS troops began heading towards Wonderland. A battle between three different groups took place, between Central who controlled Gustave's forces, Wonderland, which was protected by Freddy's powers, and STARS, who started attacking everyone. This happened while Nora took the opportunity to take Marco far south.

Nora contacted Marco with the radio from Thor's plane, saying, "Greeting, my handsome man; don't worry, you will take it where you should."

Marco said, "Stop calling me handsome; that sounds strange to me, especially from you."

Nora said "Why not, dear? Handsome is used for a man because you are the only human on this planet, so you become the most handsome man on the planet Apen."

"Oh, stop," Marco said, "I really hate Central, but is it by shooting . . . ah, never mind."

Nora answered in a rather loud voice, "My handsome Marco. That's true. Central and UW brought Dragon to our planet, they deserve to be beaten; after all, leaving the Apen planet for a century to experiment is a disgusting thing for me. STARS must also be beaten; they came first before Dragon invaded our planet . . . " Then Nora said to the Dutchman, "Mr. Dutchman, point the plane at STARS factories, I have a surprise for them, too."

Dutchman replied "OK! My lady. With pleasure! Go go go."

Their Thor planes then flew to an island in Lone Island province in the west of Grande. They arrived quickly. Dutchman took out his domestic monitoring drone and looked towards the coast of the island. Sounds like a big outdoor, and significant buildings like the palace there. The clouds are very thick, and it's raining; the waves are so strong that the view is difficult.

"What place is that?" Marco asked.

Dutchman replied "Ja ja, that is Lone Island, the wonderland of Grandeville! Used to be. Lots of crazy parties and festivals at that place before Dragon waves. Sad, sad, sad . . . Now it has become the main assembly plant of STARS."

The Dutchman pointed at Marco and said, "Come on, sir! It's Showtime!"

Dutchman carried a medium-sized Mecha assembly suit, and said, "This is my Dutchman backup, it's not small, but it's yours, meneer! What do you think?"

Marco happily wore it, but Nora then said on the radio from her home "My Marco, don't try to escape, I can activate the electric shock on the system from afar."

Dutchman and Marco left while their Thor aircrafts remained in auto-pilot mode in the sea. The rocks were steep along the busy road, but could not prevent them from going up. As seen from the sky, the STARS planes flew to Wonderland, and the city defense began to be complacent. The beach looked like deep white sand which stretched beside many old beach rides, skeletal umbrellas, and pale chairs. Dutchman preferred to pass steep cliffs to look for a secret entrance. This once beautiful island has turned into a prison island in the middle of a noisy sea and a raging sky.

Marco thought, *This is very strange; just as I walked with Gustave and in control via Alexa radio, but now it's changed, I am with a Dutchman and in Nora's control.* Then he looked at the Dutchman and asked "Where are we going? What are our goals here?"

Dutchman looked back at Marco and replied "Mr. Marco, we are going to party! We're going to destroy those bad people!"

Feeling still trapped and filled with suspicion of new people. Marco could only obey him until he got a good logical reason to run away or stay. Black coral is sharp and steep, but not a problem for both. The waves were so high that it hit the place, a dark storm made the atmosphere scary, and there was the sound of lightning everywhere. Then the towering lighthouse was visible in front of them, the abundant light swirling between the fogs. Not much longer, there was a large wall in the front surrounded by the city beach, then many abandoned beach stores that had long been left inside, looking lonely and dark.

"Welcome to Lone Island, but you won't feel alone," Marco said, as he read a welcome sign.

Dutchman reacted. "Je hebt gelijk! This place was once the Wonderland of the Grande country! I am so excited."

CHAPTER 14

They entered a gate leading to the market area in the city. The place was filled with rotten frozen fruits with preservative liquid, the colors of the cloth on the market that had turned pale, the streets that had no dust, and the lights that had been most damaged. Like a place that was abandoned but still forced to live, just like its inhabitants, creatures that lurked from inside dark rooms. Then a robot sound came from far away, saying, "Bonjour and welcome! Welcome! I'll make sure you will get an amazing pastime that is appropriate for your age!"

"I feel bad," Marco said with pity.

Dutchman was on standby, and then he said, "Masquerade is coming! They come—we'll see who is the craziest."

Then there were many Replica robots wearing party masks; their bodies had been assembled with various sharp objects and weapons. Dutchman then shot them all with machine guns in his left hand. The shot destroyed many things including objects around them.

Marco just kept quiet and didn't take action; then Nora shocked him with remote electric button from afar for a moment. Marco was surprised and asked, "Ouch! What is this, Nora? I don't know them, why should I fight them?"

Nora answered "Listen, handsome, kill those gale folk! They are savages; I am fed up with their cruel arts!"

"All right, stop shocking me," Marco said, and then he

thought, *Meh, these two groups are the same.*

Some crazy replicas named Masquerade came with terrifying bodies, like spider legs assembled on their Android bodies, had lots of swords and wore eighteenth-century party clothes on earth. Some were even wearing chainsaws and tried to cut Marco. The scenery was terrible — their shouts, their gait, and their rude behavior made a creepy atmosphere.

"This is worse than the Junker STARS robot from the trash can!" Marco said as he shot them.

The weather was stormy and dark, without lights. Marco tried to guess the position of the attacker through their scream. The Masquerade attacker came while shouting loudly; there were also those who loved crazy and killing tones. Male and female screams became noisy, and it invited more and more insane android replicas to Marco's position. The situation became very chaotic, brutal. All means were used to hurt, but they did not feel pain. Marco became the only one who felt fear; sweat filled his forehead, his heart pounded, and he saw horror around him.

"Too much! We have to retreat!" Marco said to the Dutchman.

Then Marco went backward with his Mecha.

Dutchman said "Don't back down, sir! Ha ha ha! This is very fun!"

"Hey, stop it guys! Why attack us?!" Marco yelled at the androids who attacked them.

When he was about to retreat, Marco was stuck on a wall; behind him, came a servant robot to him.

The servant robot saw with big eyeless eyes and said "What do you want to order, sir?"

Surprised, Marco did nothing, but the servant robot just kept quiet.

"No, thanks," Marco said.

A crazy spider-shaped replica robot came from behind him and slashed the servant robot while saying, "Argh! Aaaaa! allez-vous en! Ha ha!"

That crazy replica tried to attack Marco, but he managed to avoid it.

"There is something that makes these people angry!" Marco told the Dutchman.

But the Dutchman was busy fighting and surrounded. The crazy replica robot tried to slash Marco's head with a sword that was attached to her hand but failed. Marco hit her head. The mask fell, revealing the female human face replicated; the crazy robot later became embarrassed and went running from there while climbing a building.

What's wrong with them? Marco thought.

Marco then looked in the Dutchman's direction and asked again, but louder, "Hey Dutchman! Where are we going?!"

Dutchman answered, "Meneer! Sir! Sorry, I'm too excited; you go to the Lighthouse! I will keep them from behind you!"

* * *

With the help of Mecha, who looked like Mecha used by the Dutchman, Marco jumped up and down the building and the house. Crazy Replica Robots tried to shoot him with a net rope to tie him up; several shots were avoided, but some, he failed to prevent, making Marco fall on a fruit market. That made a lot of black preserve fruit fall everywhere, so the big-headed, little-headed cleaning wheeled robots came to clean the place. The servant robots then lifted the rotten fruit and put it on the carts while sweeping the tables.

Like a strange ecosystem, Marco thought, bemused.

Shortly, there came a lot of crazy replicas with spider legs and sword-arms running towards him. Their shouts made their position known, and Marco managed to dodge them. Becoming annoyed with the situation, Marco ran to avoid the chase while continuing towards the Lighthouse sitting atop the high hill. The crazy robot was in high-speed; there was one giant replica robot coming. It looked different from a crescent-shaped white mask, with two spear-shaped legs, and an old hand from a sharp sword, while wearing a Masquerade party mask. She stretched her hands quickly towards Marco. Unable to escape, Marco tried to shoot, but the crazy robot managed to dodge quickly. When he wanted to cut Marco's Mecha head, he managed to avoid it while firing back. The party robot's clothes were destroyed, and there was a naked white android body shaped like a woman's body inside.

Feet and hands from the sword? I have to be able to take off the mask, maybe it works, Marco thought while guessing.

When the crazy robot quickly attacked again, Marco tried to avoid it but failed. Mecha's left hand holding the weapon was destroyed. Marco only had one Mecha hand, and he used it to hit the crazy robot mask. The mask detached and the crazy robot ran away. But then came another crazy robot, from the type of man and woman; the insane replica robot attacked Marco again. Marco dislodged their masks, so they were embarrassed and ran away. But there were too many, Marco had to run.

"Damn!" Marco said in panic.

He saw a tall, burned restaurant building, and tried to jump past it. The jump was good, but the tall building made Marco have to enter one of the upper floors. Inside, he met several other crazy replica robots; this time they were sitting at tables. Shocked to see Marco, they used kitchen knives and threw them at him. The crazy replica robots even tried to run over Marco with chairs and tables while screaming. Without weapons to shoot, Marco moved into the next room in the restaurant, looked at the window and jumped out. But the jump was hurried and he fell into the building next to the restaurant building—an art building with the opera house, gallery and much more.

Marco fell with his Mecha into a large showroom. A little dizzy, Marco stood up and said, "Ouch, what else is this?"

A row of crescent-masked replica robots in front of him spotted him. There were about ten men and women, with sharp spear-like legs, their hands assembled into various shapes of sharp objects, such as knives, spears and even giant scissors. They had neatly-tied hair, elegant dance clothes, and they advanced quickly to catch Marco. They had no sound like other crazy replica robots, making their position challenging to know. They were climbing walls, some running straight.

Marco became afraid and said, "Nora! Dutchman! Anyone! Help me; those ballerinas aren't friendly at all!"

Nora said, "Boy, calm yourself. You can get past those crazy heel-and-toe dancers! Come on, you can do it."

"You're just as crazy as them, Nora! I don't know what your purpose was taking me to a place like this," Marco said grouchy.

Running away, Marco headed for many doors covered in red cloth, and entered another art room, this time with many mirrors, many replicas of masked naked men and women who stood posing on small platforms like they were trying to be painted.

There was the sound of the same robot again like the one on the beach; he said, "Bonjour! Welcome! Pour and mistress! Let me introduce the arts that suit your age!"

"Who is this crazy person?" Marco asked Nora through the radio.

Nora replied, "Another crazy person. I hate his art."

"Wait a minute!" Marco growled. "You sent me here just to fight your rival? You and your rival are crazy—there is no difference! This isn't even art."

Having no choice because he was going to be electrocuted, in his broken clothes, Marco had to get ready. Then the group of replica who stood naked began to release their fingering hands and replace them with metal spears in the form of sharp spears. Their feet were then inserted into pointed cone-shaped shoes; their robotic ankles bent down and entered into pointed cone shoes correctly.

Nora can see through the camera from Marco's Mecha and said, "Hah, look at how bad it is — strange heels. Weirdo."

Regardless of the incident, Marco scoffed away, then came the crescent masked replica he had found, they pierced the floor, roof, and walls. A replica attack was about to stab Marco; he then broke his hand and used it as a spear. Marco violently swung it at their masks, and even cut some heads.

"STOP, YOU GUYS!" Marco shouted, "I'm not interested in hurting you; let me go. I was forced here!"

Marco found a way out, then ran hard, leaving the place. Once outside, he got a long ladder up to the lighthouse. He jumped up and down the stairs while being chased by crazy Lone Island replicas. Finally, Marco reached the end of the stairs, found the large Lighthouse door, and entered it, locking it from inside. Crazy replicas tried to stab the door and tear it off its hinges.

* * *

Walking back to see the situation, Marco said through the radio, "Hey, Nora and Dutchman, I've arrived at the Lighthouse, now what?"

Suddenly there was a voice from inside the dark Lighthouse room, a soft sound like a little girl said, "Hallo there."

Shocked, Marco found Nora sitting on a chair while raising her feet on the table, and looked like she was relaxing. This time Nora wore a red veil and had covered her face with Calaveras or a skull paint as in the "Day of the Dead" festival.

Marco became increasingly angry and said, "What is this? You test me? Why is your face painted like that and you wear a red veil?"

Nora replied, "Listen, Dear, the festival is now a permanent thing in my new life, although I do not believe that the dead have conscious spirits. I was Little Red Riding Hood with wolves." She stood up from the chair and continued "I am happy to see your progress; you must be ready before facing Dragon."

Marco said, "Listen to me, you one-hundred-and-thirteen-years-old woman-in-the-form-of-a-child. I was ready from the start, don't waste my time! My blood is boiling enough."

Suddenly the door of the Lighthouse was destroyed, and the crazy masked replica robots then entered to find them.

Nora said "Now, Dear, we see, whose artwork is stronger? Plastic or metal?"

"That's a stupid question," Marco snarled because he didn't care.

Then Nora summoned her troops with whistles; many Redcoat robots appeared, which were made of sturdy plastic synthetics, and some were from wax. They walked down from the many lighthouse stairs. The two forces attacked each other; masked replica troops tried to cut the body of Nora's robot troops but failed, because the Redcoat robot was wrapped in solid and heavy synthetic.

"Come with me," said Nora.

Marco walked along despite his state of anger. They walked out through the back door.

Marco asked, "What about Dutchman? I did not hear the radio."

Nora replied, "Quiet, Darling, he wittingly turned off communication because he was having fun; this is not the first time we have played on this big island."

The two of them stood on a high hill while looking at the whole city. Nora pointed to the darkness and said, "Look, handsome, your friends are there, if indeed they are your friends."

"Friends? Who are they?" Marco asked.

"Gustave's forces," Nora answered. "They have descended from the east coast of this island, and we are from the west."

Marco said, "Yes, I remember. Before going to Wonderland, oh . . . sorry about that place. Gustave had the chance to deploy troops for this island."

After the fog began to slowly disappear, they saw that the massive Zeppelin from Gustave's troops were in the eastern city. Smoke and flames flared at their location, like they were at war with the island's local inhabitants.

"Who is that guy?" Marco asked. "Who has the voice of a robot through a loudspeaker in this city? Is he or she the island version of Constantine?"

Nora replied, "That kind of thing—every territory of authority must have a ruler."

"What's the name?" Marco asked again.

"Pretty lady and handsome man, that's their name," Nora answered, "They has been controlling this island for a long time."

"I only hear one voice, like a robot," Marco said.

Nora chuckled and said, "You will be surprised when you hear this."

"Not anymore," Marco said, "I've seen a lot of strange things on this planet."

Nora then replied "Because of their love, the two couples united their bodies, like becoming one flesh. I mean, one body in metal."

"Okay, grandma, got it," Marco said.

Then Nora face turned angry, hit Marco's stomach, and said, "Stop calling me grandma, Dear. I'm a robot, I'm not aging! Even I still have a child brain."

Marco replied in an angry voice, "Okay, whatever you want—a century-old robot that doesn't grow old."

While stroking his aching stomach, Marco said "Why does it hurt? I'm in Mecha armor."

Nora chuckled again and said, "Hah, of course, Darling, I prepared a special place to hit you with my hand."

"Oh, stop calling me that name. Sounds really weird!" Marco said to Nora.

Nora said "Dear Marco, if you fail to defeat the Dragon or retreat then I will make you a replica. Just make sure your brain is not destroyed when hit by a dragon or anyone; we will live together forever."

From afar came the Dutchman, Mecha's body looked like he was from a great fight, with many pieces of sharp objects like knives and holes around his Mecha body.

Dutchman then said "My lady! Good news! I know the position of the two damn artists! Yes, ha ha ha!"

"Where are they, buddy?" Asked Nora.

Dutchman pointed in the direction of the city center. "There! Over there! In the middle of the city, precisely in a five-star hotel there."

"GIVE ME MY LITTLE BIRD ARMOR!" Nora shouted to one of the Redcoat robots she had created.

Then they brought a winged Mecha assembled with jet power.

"Both of you, jump towards that place! I will fly," Nora said. She flew up with the Mecha desert.

"What about their net shots?" Marco asked, but the Dutchman and Nora had already left.

Finally, Marco also jumped in, too, passing the Lone Island

city buildings vigilantly.

The sound of the loudspeaker was heard again. It said: "Oh, my visitors are very stubborn! Your courage will be a pleasant spectacle; enjoy my City of Art! This city is my art!"

While continuing to jump up and down with his Mecha, Marco thought, *Oh shit, why do replicas here love to follow their crazy leaders? That's ridiculous.*

While walking on the roof of the buildings, Marco looked down to find many crowds of crazy masked replicas who followed him from the road on the ground. They piled up one another like a collection of insects below. Their legs were like two-legged spiders, and some were even six-legged, stepping on one another and injuring each other. As he continued to run above the long building, suddenly a masked replica robot came out of the roof, trapping Marco, and pulled him down. The masked robot then laughed while trying to tear apart the armor body of Marco's Mecha. Marco quickly kicked him until he was thrown out the window.

"LEAVE ME ALONE, YOU FREAK!" Marco shouted.

The robot came back again. From the top floor balcony, he shot the point of his spears legs and thrust one of Marco's Mecha legs.

"Damn, what else is this? My robotic leg was pierced," Marco said.

Marco tried to jump again and came out on the roof. He then jumped harder into the next building because the Dutchman and Nora had walked away. But the trip was so severe—the buildings in the city were designed in a classic style and in the form of a variety of Victorian-style architectures. As he continued walking, Marco finally arrived at the hotel park he was headed for. When he was about to step into the garden, he saw that the garden was not planted with plants, but with sculptures. Suddenly the Mechanical robot was bound to black metal threads that were not visible because of the darkness of the place covered in clouds. Then the crazy replica in masks came out from among the sculptures in the sculpture garden — with the bodies of spider-shaped metal-robotic robots with many hands that shoot needles with metal thread ends.

"Someone help," Marco said, trapped. "I can't go forward, and my Mecha is tied to the trap in these metal threads."

Nora turned around, as she flew, she shot at the robots that had tied Marco and released him.

"Good for a little old woman!" Marco said, detaching himself from the threads and advancing. He had to step on many carved statues because he had no other way.

Nora said, "My dear, do you have hatred for the statues?"

"No," Marco replied. "They just blocked my way."

He finally arrived and entered through the hotel door. After going into the spacious living room, Marco saw the Dutchman trapped in thicker and larger metal threads.

"SIR, leave me here. I can deal with it. HURRY UP AND SET THIS UP!" shouted Dutchman.

CHAPTER 15

When Marco was about to move, a giant replica measuring five meters high appeared, with a spider body that had many threads and masked four heads; the assembled robot had a blue water tube behind it.

"Oh, look, another strange thing," Marco said.

The same sound came from the nearest speaker, he said "Strange? Ha ha! That's the great thing about my art!"

"Looks like we have different tastes," Marco said to the voice.

"Very disappointing," the voice said. "Our visitors are not interested, but really want to meet me. Sorry, I do not provide my signature for someone who does not like my art."

Before Marco could answer, the eight-legged spider robot attacked him, trying to tie his Mecha with a more massive thread . . . and it worked.

"No, no more!" Marco said.

He then saw the spider approaching with masks on each of its heads; it had been assembled from four replica bodies so that it had four heads. Marco tried to take his hand out and take off the masks, but failed — the masks were sewn on their faces. No more weapons and the Dutchman was still trapped, and Marco was trapped inside the threads.

Marco looked behind him, trying to find Nora and contacted her on the radio, saying, "Nora, where are you? You've taken us this far; now we're trapped."

Nora and her Mecha birds flew through a large window and shot the head of the giant spider. One of the masks was half broken, then the replica head who lost half of her mask began to lower her head feeling embarrassed and crying hysterically, her long hair covering her face. Nora shots the other head to destroy the mask and succeeded. One more head lost his mask because it was damaged, and he began to rebel hysterically because his face was visible.

"Very good!" Marco said excitedly.

"Yeah, that's Nora for you, ha ha ha!" Nora said on the radio, laughing.

The big spider then got out of control, the four heads hysterically clashed and attacked each other. They cried hysterically and then walked backward. Marco slipped from the thread because the ties weren't too strong. The Dutchman was still trapped.

Dutchman said, "Oh, sir! My Lady! I'm still stuck, please?"

Then from inside the hotel that had many doors, came out other strange robotic creatures; this time they had a painting attached to the neck of his head held in both hands, walking on two legs.

"What's more? Your taste is awful!" Marco said in a voice while offending him.

The voice replied, "Hah, L.O.L. I'm laughing out loud. See the power of my arts! Enjoy the next strange show!"

Then more robots came out. This time they came out in various shapes; some had lights on their heads, some were covered in linen, some had half sculptures, some were combined with musical instruments like big trumpets, and some had much more weird costumes.

Seeing the freaks replicas coming toward him, Marco said, "Stop it, aren't you embarrassed?"

The voice then said, "Shame?! This is beautiful art! You're just an art hater, you don't know anything!"

Getting annoyed, Marco said, "Art? I don't care about your style, but using violence is a corrupt one! You are just a collection of maniacs who don't know what true art means."

The voice said, "Pour de vrai? I am the greatest artist on the planet! Then what does true art mean?"

"A work of beauty and emotional power in a rational way. You have a wrong artistic passion," Marco answered.

"It seems we have a different art path. Is there anything more perfect than merging our unspeakable emotion and unbearable lust together in passion?" The voice continued, "Every person has a different taste; why? We are just robots, we don't really have a sense of lust nor pain. There are no rules to follow here, I will bring my imagination to motion in any way. I am a free man."

"But your works cry! They hate themselves! It is dirty art, you have failed to become an artist!" Marco said.

Nora, from a distance clapped her hands. She said to them with a big voice from above the balcony, "Amazing! He's the first and the last visitor who hates your work, don't you know? That means you failed? He is the only human! Ha ha ha ha!"

Then the crazy robotic forces all retreated, re-entered the doors because they were controlled by the sound. Then after a moment of silence, a door opened.

The door opened, and a replica appeared. They're merged between a couple, from two sexes between men and women. They are the voice.

They say, "An art needs criticism; as an artist, I have to accept it. Seems like we have a new rules here."

Seeing that person, Marco became confused and said "All right, I think we're finished here. Nora, can we leave now?"

Nora went down with her bird robot and said, "Finish? This loser has tortured many replicas; he must be punished by law!"

The person said again, "Law? We don't have one, Nora? I

don't think that the lifeless use one."

Nora replied, "Then I will make sure that you will become truly lifeless! Hah!"

Nora took out a scythe that was longer than her body.

"Wait, what's that for?" Marco asked. "Let him fix this place as a punishment; that's quite worth it, enough bloodshed, oh . . . I mean oil from murder between robots."

The person said again, "Wait? That's right, sir, whoever your name is. You have no problem because my army has retreated. Gustave's robots, your alliance, can come here."

"Oh, that's good," Marco said.

Nora then threw the scythe. Marco was just a little hit. Nora said, "How many times should I tell you? They are just Central accomplices, those who have killed your friends! Stay with me; we will beat everyone, including Dragon!"

Marco said, "Then? You say there are STARS headquarters here with their factories! Where? I didn't see them; you lied to me, too. You made fun of me from the start!"

Seeing the increasingly chaotic situation, the person said, "Listen to me, ladies and gentlemen. Regarding the factory, it was moved ten years ago by STARS, when Grande lost a lot of Replicas because it protected a human. It made STARS became afraid of Dragon. Then I was forced to make a deal so that I could calmly take control of this island."

"Agreement? Huh?" asked Nora.

The person replied, "STARS gave me the power to control all replicas on this island, while I'm protecting their factories that are hidden around this island."

"Then where are they? Don't waste my time!" Nora said angrily.

The person pointed out the balcony, towards the sea, "There, at sea."

They all walked towards the balcony, then saw green lights from the seawater; between the waves, the green lights began to appear.

"That's them! You call them, don't you?" Nora said to the person.

The person answered in a half-male-female voice, saying, "We have no choice, we are cornered, and your position is known, but look! At least what you are looking for are coming to find you."

"You guys are pathetic, you make friends with enemies of our old world, and you are a member of STARS. You work together with them, so they gave you lots of technology to control this desolate island, and its replicas . . . but, but I forgive you," Nora said.

With enthusiasm, the person said, "Good! Felicitazione! I will correct my mistakes; I accept your criticism. I will make sure my future arts will more friendly!"

Before they finished, Nora had taken the sickle, and then cut the person's head off; the body and heads then fell from the balcony into the cliff to the beach.

"What?" Marco asked in surprise, "You had just forgiven them!"

Nora laughed and said, "Ha ha ha ha! Relax, darling. Finally, I became the most influenced artist on the planet! Now let's leave this junk place."

"Wait a minute!" Marco said "You said we would attack STARS! Now back off? Okay, I agree."

Nora replied, "Take it, easy, darling, no need to rush. After all, there are Gustave troops here; let them attack STARS—we can possibly win."

Then Nora pulled Marco and Dutchman away, but, behind them was an extensive collection of large-headed assembled robots, wearing large helmets and green uniforms. They were Gustave's troops.

One of the robots advanced and said, while looking at Marco,

"You are here? Monsieur, the colonel has been looking for you everywhere."

"No! No!" Nora said, "He belongs to my group, you failed ten years ago, now let me have a chance."

"Unauthorized authorization, one of the citizens of Wonderland, hostile detected," said the robot, then pointed their weapons at Nora and Dutchman's faces.

"STOP IT GUYS! They are not hostile, I ordered you to hold the fire!" Marco shouted.

Suddenly a rocket burst from the sea and hit the place. The hotel collapsed and all the soldiers who were inside sprinted out. From the sea there appeared more bright green lights, and from underwater, STARS troops emerged one by one, with robotic bodies that had many modifications and cables. Cyborg corpses were revived with the Exoskeleton.

"Oh, look," said Nora, "Corpse in the shell is coming."

Marco's Mecha was severely damaged, so Dutchman helped get him out. It was time to make a decision, between following Nora or Gustave's troops.

Nora said, "Listen, darling, the replica of the robot that I cut his neck was named Alphonse Constant; with his wife, they were a doll of STARS."

Marco asked, "So? Why do we have to fight STARS? We go straight to the southern country."

"STARS? They are my goal, too," Nora answered.

"Why? Isn't Dragon killing everyone including you?" Marco asked.

Hearing those words, Nora replied, "STARS is responsible for making the planet's defenses weak; they are also the culprit of the world war, getting us to fight each other while they're watching from space. STARS then came and killed many people, including my parents! But dragons were unexpected—they came down to Apen and scorched everyone."

Still, Marco had to make a decision. Gustave's troops returned to him after the ruins of the hotel building and asked, "Monsieur, the colonel wants to talk to you by phone, are you willing?"

Marco turned to look at Nora and said, "Give me time, I have to talk to Gustave or Alexa."

Marco quickly picked up the phone that Gustave's army robot had given him and spoke. Apparently it was Gustave's voice. Marco said, "Hello, Colonel, answer honestly, who are you? Are you part of Central? Is your brain also an android brain? And is Alexa ... is he also from Central? Answer now."

Gustave replied "Hello sir! Nice to hear you are still alive. We must immediately go to the south; everything has been prepared."

"Don't change the conversation, Colonel! Answer honestly. I already know everything."

After a pause of about five seconds, Alexa's voice was then heard from the phone.

"Alexa? You are still alive," Marco sounded relieved.

Alexa said, "Listen to me, Marco. Nora must have said all that, but you know, I did work with Central, but I am not a Central AI; I am a replica created with the technology between UW and Central. I am a replica of a previous human named Alexa, I am Alexa."

"Okay, maybe, but don't lie to me—sooner or later, I will know? Then what about Gustave?" Marco asked.

Alexa answered from the phone, she said, "Unfortunately, Nora is right for this one; Gustave is an old robot with a brain from AI Central. But believe me, we don't know about your friends. Central just told us to take you to Dragon and kill it."

"I will go to that place," Marco replied, "but not with your help. You are friends of my enemy, so I have to go with your enemy."

Nora said from behind, "Good! Good, darling! Let's go!"

Then Marco turned around, left the phone and joined Nora and Dutchman. As they were about to leave, the STARS robotic corpses that were reassembled, revived from the Dead Sea. Those cyborg walked with many glowing green robotic eyes on their head, deep from the dark water. The sharp metal army looked rusty along with their bodies. Then from far out, giant robots shaped like a massive fortress with four legs rose from the sea. In the midst of high waves, strong winds, and lightning, the Leviathan robots raised from the sea.

"Is that our next target?" Marco asked.

Nora replied, "That, Darling, is our destination! STARS factories that continue to redesign troops to control the planet."

Gustave's sky troops began attacking the STARS troops who had just come out of the sea. Zeppelin and the assembled aircraft started flying above the ocean but the STARS defense was more robust—they shot back with large laser beams into the sky. Their big lasers, like they were smoldering, make everything around shine because of the reflection of light. Green lights mixed with red rose to the sky, shooting the planes above.

"DUTCHMAN!" Shouted Nora.

"Yes, my lady! Ahoy!" Dutchman answered with joy.

Nora said, "Give your Mecha to Marco, I will attack the factories with him!"

"Eh, but . . . ah, all right, my lady! With pleasure! Please!" The Dutchman responded with a tired face.

"Marco!—I mean, darling—let's go in there," Nora said to Marco after Dutchman left his Mecha.

Seeing that Marco was going to follow Nora, Alexa raised the volume of his phone from one of Gustave's army robots and said, "Monsieur Marco. No, we beg you. You can die there; don't be crazy. We are close to our common goal. Come back."

"No, Alexa," Marco replied. "Didn't you say I have to help

this dead planet? I'll do it my way."

Then, along with Nora, Marco went to STARS troops who arrived.

The Dutchman Mecha used by Marco was more deadly. When Mecha issued an immense turbo power command, it made Marco fly under control from Nora. He then jumped very high towards the STARS factory on the beach, a walking fortress.

* * *

The high jump shocked Marco; he fell right above the enormous dark giant robot, called the Factory. Marco said, "No wonder the Dutchman is faster than me—his Mecha is very great."

Nora flew above and said, "Darling, come with me, we are looking for an entrance; our small size old robots are difficult to detect."

Nora then landed near Marco. He spotted a large glass and shot it to pieces. It took dozens of shots before finally the durable glass was destroyed and a way opened for Marco to enter the factory.

"What's inside this big robot, I mean this factory?" Marco asked.

"You will know," Nora answered.

Seeing Marco's position in danger, Alexa and Gustave sent more of the army to attack STARS to divert their attention. Marco and Nora entered through the broken glass, finding a dark room. A Flying Mecha bird used by Nora folded her wings and quickly changed her shape to something like a wolf.

Being surprised that Marco was amazed, Nora said, "This is what I mentioned as the Little Red Riding Hood."

Then the wolf Mecha emitted red light from his eyes, and

Marco could see in the dark, thanks to the advanced Mecha she has.

Her treatment confused Marco and he wanted to ask, but Nora replied "Oh, this lamp makes you confused? This is to divert attention; your Mecha is strong enough. Enter yourself."

Lightless hallways, lots of cables and oil, and smelled like salts. The place was very dark like a rat's aisle, and there was plenty of strange machines sounds like sharp, thunderous sounds from a computer. Quietly, Marco advanced to find another large room, this time a storage room, where he saw many glass tubes and human brains scattered on the floor. Then there were the letters of light on the walls, with sea-green color, lit amid hardships.

Marco wanted to vomit to see those chunks of flesh. *Oh, people still use cables nowadays, also this makes me ill! Look at the brains, it looks so thick even though it is frozen."*

Nora said, "Dear, don't be sick; STARS is moving the memory of the cyborg human brains and their cyborg aliens into the AI machines' brains. So this is where the origin of their memory is—unlike us who bury corpses politely after copying their brains."

"Polite?" Marco said. "The Underworld under the city of Wonderland is a catacomb containing bones. I am sure you have different terms for graves . . . very strange."

Nora answered, "Still better, do you see the sand along the island of Lone? Before the war there was no sand here; it came from bones burned by Alphonse Constant. His statues are also made of the same ash."

Suddenly, the STARS guard found them. This time was the same type of robot named Junker, a poorly assembled robot that had many fingers. Marco quickly destroyed them, until they piled up to form a junk hill.

"We have to find the robot! Stop wasting time, "said Nora.

"Which robot is it?" Marco asked, looking at Nora.

Nora pointed in various directions, "I don't know, but the controller robot that activates all the STARS sleeping machines is leading the STARS military operation from cadaver and wreckage."

Marco then advanced leaving Junker who kept trying to fight him with his bare hands.

Later, accidentally, he arrived at the production room, where there were many baby bones. "Ah, what is this place?" Marco asked.

Nora didn't answer, so Marco said, "Oh, so the myth is true. Star Ranger gets Cyborg troops from breeding meat through machines; these babies must be stolen and collected from various colonies. They not only made loyal cyborg from volunteers and slaves, but also from babies. This is very vile."

"This is the kind of evil arts that must be destroyed from existence," Nora said.

A hoot happened inside; Gustave's troops managed to bomb STARS several times.

Nora said, "We must hurry! Come on!"

Marco rushed in and out of different rooms looking for the place where the controller robot was located. They then saw a point of light from far away.

"That must be where the robot is," Marco said.

The two of them quickly went there without getting significant resistance from a wave of STARS worker robots named Junker. They walked on the giant cables that led to the place to arrive at the light spot.

CHAPTER 16

But their entry was blocked by a locked door. Marco saw some mathematical symbols he didn't understand. "This must be the code; we need to press the right password button," Marco said.

Nora said, "Don't waste your time—calculating Star Ranger numbers are different from humans. There are many types of numbers— things like one to seven, some have unlimited symbols, there are numbers that are symbolic of sound signals, and so on. It takes incredible logic to be able to read their system according to its type."

"So now what? Can you solve this one? How to break the codes?"

"Dear, you like to ask too many questions. Break the codes you ask? Here's how," Nora answered, and then she blew the door with a bomb.

The door opened easily. Marco looked inside. There was a factory control center room with lots of monitors and texts. They also saw a standard thin body robot there.

"Is that it? The controller? He looks silly." Marco said.

Nora answered, "Yes."

Marco said "But? You're kidding, right? Is this the one who raised them?"

Nora replied, "Right, this robot is one of the survivors after the plasma wave from the Dragon shook the planet. The robot who was responsible for awakening STARS troops from their deaths. I know this story from people."

"Well, I think one hit is enough," Marco said, advancing towards the skinny robot.

The robot was shocked to see them, and then said, "It's bad! It's bad! Emergency! Emergency! Intruder! Intruder!"

Marco said confidently, "Hah, that's right; nobody will save you. All your troops are on the beach and also in northern Wonderland. But, Nora I feel sorry for him, are you sure this is their leader?"

Then the skinny robot went to pull a tube nearby, taking much effort. The robot banged on the glass tube while saying, "Help! Please! I will!! Be Beaten! Beaten! Beaten so hard in pain!"

The tube was written CF556.

"You are slow! Let me beat him!" Nora said as she stepped forward past Marco.

When Nora started to cut the skinny robot's head with the long sickle she was carrying, suddenly the glass tube broke, and the thin robot was thrown away. Nora backed away, thinking there was an explosion.

A mysterious figure came out of the tube accompanied by a lot of white smoke like a gas that had evaporated. It was the Cyborg Captain, dubbed as the Wasp by UW, with STARS masks, thin futuristic armor and wings behind it that used supersonic speed power. A female cyborg figure came out, with a corpse face, black hair, the body of a cyborg robot, and a replica of STARS that rose from a long sleep. Seen before wearing her clothes, there were many strange letters along the skin, glowing with the spring-green color over her body made of dark metal.

Nora said, "Marco, step down—she must be the Wasp army, the most dangerous type of cyborg female in the sky."

The Wasp came out of the tube in full armor, then took out two green-energy, medium-sized swords, like bright green fireflies flying between her bodies—a small machine that perfected her weapon. Looking at Marco without saying anything, the Wasp threw one of her swords, the energy sword swirling and flying like a drone she controlled, slicing through various objects and walls. Marco and Nora had a chance to avoid it, but the sword flew everywhere, distracting them. That's when Wasp came forward and stabbed Nora. The energy sword used by the Wasp penetrated the Mecha wolf and injured her.

"No! Nora! HEY YOU, FIGHT ME!" Marco shouted testily.

The Wasp's sword stuck on Nora Mecha, and the other sword flew back into her hand. Marco shot at the Wasp, but she able to dodge it quickly, moving like smoke. Marco took the opportunity to catch Nora Mecha and jump fly to take her away from there.

Nora regained consciousness and said, "No darling, I'm just a burden; go to the surface! Look for other help. I don't know if there is a Wasp that can still be replicated!"

Nora let go of Marco, and his Mecha jumped too strong to make it to the factory roof.

* * *

Marco fell on a broad platform above the robot factory. Wasp suddenly appeared again, and this time she called many other swords to fly with her—the Wasp held six swords at once in both hands. The rain made it slippery. Gustave's army tried to shoot that robot factory, but their legs were too strong even for bombs because they were coated with various super-strong layers. While Marco was trapped, he tried to jump again, but he was worried that Nora is still trapped inside the factory.

Marco then stood with his Mecha and said to Wasp, "All right, captain! Come on, if you really want to hurt me."

Without a word, the Wasp ran towards Marco. Marco tried to shoot and hit back, but the Wasp was very agile. Wasp managed to cut his Mecha hands, then his two swords stabbed both of Marco's Mecha legs, so he was jammed. Marco managed to swat the Wasp away, but the Wasp then transformed his sword into a gun and shot at Marco repeatedly. That caused severe damage to his Mecha's body.

Oh no. I'm stuck, Marco thought, then he looked up and around him, looking for a way out.

As he walked closer, the Wasp stopped and tilted his head while looking at Marco inside Mecha.

"You win, I lose. My Mecha robot is stuck. Stop, this is Nora's idea, not mine; release me, please," Marco begged Wasp.

Suddenly Nora appeared behind him, holding the skinny robot. The Wasp was surprised and looked back.

Nora said "Let him go! Or I hurt your leader." While holding her scythe on the skinny robot's neck, Nora threatened the Wasp.

The Wasp only saw it while not moving—like she didn't care. Then came the other STARS troops; using ship chains they climbed to the factory roof to find Marco and Nora. The cyborg robots looked weak and rusty—not very strong—but their body is bulletproof. Wasp seemed somewhat surprised to see his friends. Marco realized something, so he took out a mirror that Nora had given him and showed it to the Wasp.

Marco said, "Look, your beautiful face! Happy hundred year's birthday."

The Wasp cyborg's eyes then glowed big, like looking at a haunt; she suddenly threw away her sword and held her face. The wasp tried to say something, but her voice sounded sick like she was choking.

The wasp then shouted. Her voice was very sharp and loud as if mixed with the creepy scream of a damaged computer, which shattered her vocal cords. The voice came to Gustave's troops who then headed for their position by plane. Gustave's pilot forces then scattered rain of bullets at the STARS troops who were above the walking factory.

Marco took the opportunity to get out of his Mecha and head for Nora. Nora put the skinny robot into her storage space in her Mecha wolf, while providing another seat for Marco to sit on.

"Why do you bring this skinny robot?" Marco asked.

"I want its knowledge—this is for intelligence!" Nora answered.

Nora then flew with Marco away from the roof of the factory-legged robot. Marco noticed that there was a hole in Nora's chest.

"Nora," Marco asked, "Where are we going? Your wound looks bad—I can see the hole through to the back of your Mecha."

Nora said, "Take it easy, sir, you can't really kill the dead."

When they were about to fly back to the shore, Nora blew up the legged factory with a bomb she had installed, but an unexpected occurrence occurred. Wasp flew to Nora's Mecha wings and shot them with a weapon that was held in his hand. Nora turned around with her Mecha and shot back, but the bullet was too slow to hit the Wasp.

"Hold on, dear! We will fall!" Nora said.

"Try to fall in the right place!" Marco said fearfully.

Nora turned and said, "Take it!"

Feeling confused, Marco asked, "Take it? What do you mean?"

"I will distract her from you, it seems like there is a clutter of love in her eyes towards you," Nora said to him.

Nora gave the Mecha steering wheel to Marco, and flew out with a jetpack in her bag; carrying a long scythe and a large revolver, she flew in search of the Wasp. Seeing the Mecha plane falling, the Wasp flew to one of Gustave's Zeppelin to monitor. Nora followed her. Wasp turned to see Nora. The wind was extreme in the clouds. Gustave's assembled planes saw that and chased them while flying between the Zeppelins waiting for the right time because they were afraid to shoot their own Zeppelins.

The Wasp saw Nora and said in a machine sound that was not understood—referred to as a synth-wave language, the language of the Star Ranger faction.

Nora asked, while pointing and threatening, "Hey, who are you talking to?"

The Wasp looked toward the sky and she called STARS aircraft forces through their own communication signal. They came and hit Gustave's patrol aircraft. Nora then shot at the Wasp but missed the swift target. While trying to play with Nora, the Wasp threw two glowing green swords, which flew in the sky around Nora. The Wasp then advanced with four swords on her hands and waist.

"If you think my sickle is just a decoration, then you are wrong, you ugly demon!" Nora said and made the tip of the crescent detach, holding it like a metal chain in her hands. Nora then turned it to cut the flying Wasp swords.

Unconsciously, the metal rope from the spinning sickle wrapped around the Wasp's body. Nora drained electricity to injure the Wasp. Seeing herself bound, she shot the Wasp, which made the Wasp angry, who cut the chain and damaged Nora's sickle. The Wasp sword was too sharp. Only the handle of the weapon remained, but it could be explosive because it was designed by Nora. When the Wasp advanced, she summoned his swords to fly again—this time four flying swords attacked Nora. As she approached, Nora threw a bomb and fled. The explosion didn't hurt Wasp at all because avoided it. Nora flew to the Zeppelin wing, where she entered to get the Gustave robot army. The wasp was burned severely, but she just stood there unfazed.

The assembled Gustave's robots said, "Lady, raise your hands—you've been surrounded!"

"Not me," said Nora, "but she is what you have to worry about." Nora then pointed at the green light emerging from the mist.

The Wasp had followed Nora.

"Good, I successfully baited her," Nora said.

* * *

Wasp came into the Zeppelin; every one shot at her immediately because she looked dangerous, but she used her swords to slow down the army of Gustave's assembled army robots. The Wasp continued to follow Nora who entered the stairs to the wheelhouse. Because it was small, Nora was hardly visible; it was easier for her to cover without being shot. The Wasp chased her while chopping lots of robots with her swords. Nora closed the metal doors, but the Wasp cut it quickly like paper.

"Fire bullets," said Nora, while replacing the magazine for her revolver.

The Wasp entered, cutting the iron wall just big enough to find Nora. Nora then shot her with a fire flare bullet; the Wasp dodged but could not avoid the explosion of fire that burned the place. Nora repeatedly shot her, and the Wasp ducked, but the explosions burned all areas including the Wasp. Nora then looked for the window and jumped out, but one of the flying swords slashed her left hand and broke it. Nora fell to the floor, the Wasp quickly ran forward, stabbing a hole in Nora's stomach. Wasp then shouted at Nora, but Nora lifted her gun filled with fire bullets, took the opportunity, and shot the Wasp's mouth. The Wasp's head caught on fire, and she then ran aimlessly until she was trapped. Without the use of her left hand, Nora flew away. The big Zeppelin then burned entirely and fell down to the sea. The Wasp lost her balance burned in that place, dying with a final scream.

Marco managed to fly away and get to the beach. He found the Dutchman already bound, but he was hampered by Gustave's robot army in a field.

They flashed Marco's plane to shoot with lights. Marco then flew low and landed it away from them.

They pointed their weapons at him and said, "Sorry, sir, but you must come with us."

They were taking him to one of the transport planes, but the aircraft was destroyed by a rocket from afar. Then the island's crazy robots were controlled by STARS AI. White replica eyes turned into red lights, becoming fully controlled under STARS. Without shame, insane replica robots with sharp hands advanced to attack. From the coast came a corpse mixed with STARS cyborg robots that were rusty and full of horror from the light of their eyes and mouth. Automatically, the flying wolf aircraft that Marco used earlier launched a flare-up. Not long after the Nora-assembled Robot troops made of sturdy mixed synthetic came. Redcoat-style soldiers sprang up from the other side. With bolt-action weapons, the robotic Redcoats tried to come to protect Marco and Dutchman at Nora's orders.

Without protection from Mecha's armor, Marco said "Eh, sorry. Isn't there another way to protect me?"

Too busy processing a lot of information from the events around, the robots did not answer. Bullets came from various directions, the atmosphere became chaotic, and crazy replica forces tore apart everything, while Gustave robots were cornered back in one direction. The field had a lot of glowing streetlights that revealed everyone's position. Fewer Redcoat troops were initially torn apart by waves of STARS troops who came like a flood. The scream of robots and the sound of shattered metal brought an atmosphere of horror to the event.

Dutchman then ran from there with his hands tied, and Dutchman shouted in Marco's direction. He said "MISTER MARCO, I WILL COME BACK AGAIN! SEE YOU LATER! I HAVE TO GO!! GOOD LUCK."

The Dutchman then put on the Nora wolf plane parked and left there because it was broken from the Wasp attack before. Gustave's robots armies that protects Marco was cornered at a place in the city that leads to the sea. Suddenly a plane appeared from the sky shooting crazy robots controlled by STARS forces; the shot burned the place like a dragon's breath.

"Ah, Napalm Strike! Came at the right time," Marco said.

It was identified as a Chasseur plane, the Grande's most expensive airplane.

Alexa then contacted Marco by phone, "Allô, Monsieur; sorry I'm late. I hope you don't run away again. We have a mission, but the fire can't hold them for very long. You have to leave. Okay?"

Alexa then landed the spacejet plane near that place, and they took Marco away with the Chasseur. Once on the flight, he saw that there was no pilot on the seat.

Marco said, "Hello? Is there anyone there?"

The voice of Alexa replied, "Hello Monsieur; Nora's nuclear almost killed me, so I moved my conscious mind to this plane before the explosion. I am the plane now."

"Wow, you are the first living fighter jet," Marco said, "That's so sexy! But I'm sorry, too—I can't stop the nuclear. Where are we going?"

Alexa replied, "Head to the south; complete the mission. I don't want you to run away again. I know you don't like Central, but you have no choice—help yourself and me, Monsieur. This time, no Central robot will join our operation."

While their planes were flying fast, they continued talking.

"So what happens when we arrive?" Marco asked.

Alexa replied, "We attack!"

Marco said, "And that's what Central wants; I don't like it. I prefer the Nora way—she wants us to talk."

Alexa became annoyed and said, "No, Monsieur! Are you crazy? Do you want to talk to monsters that destroy my entire planet? No, I will be an opponent—with or without you. My job is just to take you there."

Marco proceeded to go sit in the empty pilot's seat, because Alexa was the plane.

He said, "Do you know? I have loved planes since I was a child; beautiful planes reminded me of Monica. Too bad I have to lose her. Central shit!"

"Be careful," said Alexa, "I can feel your body's movements because this plane has a sensor."

"Oh, so you can feel me?" Marco said, "What if I kiss the steering gear; could you feel it, too?"

Marco then jokingly kissed and licked the steering gear.

"What's this, Monsieur? Control yourself; stop being silly," said Alexa.

Marco continued to do so by laughing and saying, "You haven't been in a relationship for a hundred years, have you? Come on, I'm just joking; this must be very funny. Don't tell me; I'm just trying to cheer you up."

Alexa said, "Oh, I'm glad you're still angry, Monsieur Marco. But, of course, you can do it again, it tickles me; I like it."

Marco became agitated and kept silent, but then replied, "Uhm, it's weird. Forget it; let's go to our destination. Is it that mountain?"

"Hold on," said Alexa. "It's too dangerous, we'll meet the replica army from the southern countries that Lisa has collected."

"Oh, yeah—right. I almost forgot Lisa; so she succeeded. Not like I failed in the northern countries," Marco said.

After half an hour of flying, they arrived at a southern country with what is left from the ruins of the Kingdom of Rozenland, one of the small states in the southern hemisphere. They landed on an open valley. In that area, there were no buildings, only burned woods, and mostly dunes. Not far from the landing, a door opened from the ground floor; many armored vehicles came out, one of which was a large tank called the Mini Panzer.

"What is that?" Marco asked.

Alexa replied, "That is a mini panzer."

"Mini? The panzer is twenty meters tall!" Marco said.

The vehicles surrounded their planes. A replica appeared and said, "Sorry, we thought you were Freddy's troops from the north."

Marco got off the plane and greeted them.

CHAPTER 17

A replica meet Marco and said "Welcome, who the hell are you guys?" While pointing his gun at Marco head.

Alexa said by radio to the replica, "Listen, as we talked about before, this is the man I promised."

The replica soldier was shocked and said "Wow! Are you human? I almost can't believe it" He then held Marco's face.

Marco asked "Eh, what are you doing? You can't feel my skin."

He was sad and replied, "Oh, it's a shame. Yes, sir, I don't have any sense; I'm just a cheap Android robot in the form of a human. They sent many planes to the south and were led by a general named Boneheart. He has killed many of our guards, so we have to hide in the ground, waiting for your arrival."

They then put everything into the ground; the Chasseur plane was pulled by the mini Panzer inside, too. Below the underground, there are large bunkers and long passageways.

"Welcome to Rozenland!" said a replica.

Many water pipes were there. The place was like a dumping place under the dunes that was transformed into a giant military headquarters. There were lots of garages and airplanes there.

"Oh, look, Alexa—lots of planes here," Marco said, pointing to the southern planes there.

Alexa replied "Oh? I became jealous, Monsieur. Don't you want to ride me again?"

"What? Hahaha . . . Stop teasing me. No, it's too dangerous;

we're both important. It would be a shame if we both were to die with one shot," Marco said.

Alexa react, "Oh. I'm just joking, Monsieur. Please choose the best plane they can offer; we will go to the mountain tomorrow morning. Yes?"

"Good!" Marco said.

Marco then was taken to the barracks. There were many beds and they then let him sleep there.

* * *

Many captains and generals from the southern countries gathered and they talked.

One of the generals said, "Star Ranger, Freddy, and now Nora, oh . . . whoever the child is, they will be very troublesome."

Others said, "Are you sure, ladies and gentlemen? This is very dangerous. What if we fail again? Remember ten years ago—UW and Central lost hundreds of thousands of soldiers, and only Lee could enter. Grande lost all of their replica soldiers trying to get Lee out but even then failed and Lee died."

Gustave's brain, which was there without Marco's knowledge, was transferred to the big, robust Mecha. A brand new body with stronger defense and power.

He said in the meeting with a more sinister voice. "We no longer need a mass military operation to bring Marco in, after the meteor fell at Wonderland, Central can sent a message; according to their satellite on outer space, Prince Power are surrounded Marco to protect him at all this time."

"What? So the prince are friendly to him?" asked someone.

Gustave continued, "Exactly, Marco was brought in here with a clear intention. He was descended from the prince's daughter, one of the survivors before the plasma wave. The prince had a daughter who was Marco's grandmother, who was taken out and immigrated to Nova Anglia colonies before the war. It took us a long time—about ten years—to track them down. Unfortunately, only Marco is left from his family."

"So what? He has a family relationship with the prince? If he even exist at the first place," someone said there.

Gustave said, "Isn't that clear, gentlemen? The prince let Marco into the planet. Nobody can enter without being scorched by Phoenix in the atmosphere—except Lee with many deaths—and Marco is allowed because he's blood offspring. We will use him to defeat the Prince, avenge us, and release us from this dead planet's prison."

The replicas which were in the room became excited and happy.

Another replica general said, "Good, Sir Gustave. But . . . How do we do it, and what will we do to the Prince's only descendant after we've succeeded?"

Gustave replied, "I plan to tell you tomorrow; just prepare yourself. Regarding the death after the prince's death—if successful, I don't really care about him."

"Yes, there is also Boneheart with troops from the north; they want to destroy Marco and also us," said another person.

Gustave laughed and said "HA, HA, HA, HA, my fellow robotic masters. Just like fighting a Star Ranger or STARS—you know what is being done, and you shoot back anything that's hostile. Constantine tried to deceive me; he said he would cooperate but instead shot Marco when he wanted to meet him. Now he is dead, but his generals are attacking us. Bunch of morons."

The meeting was quickly concluded, with all returning to their separate posts, preparing for tomorrow's preparations which were only twelve hours Apen time or twenty-four hours of earth time away.

The next morning, the weather in the southern region of the planet was darker and colder than the northern part where the red moon was illuminating. Someone came to wake Marco, who was fast asleep.

"Good morning sir; you seem to sleep soundly even a day before entering the war," said the Replica soldier.

Marco just smiled; he was taken to the runway, where he could choose which planes he wanted; they even offered modification as he wished, quickly but thoroughly.

Alexa spoke to Marco on the radio from her plane. She said, "Hey, Monsieur, bonjour; have you chosen the right fighter? Today will be awful."

"Don't worry, we can do this," Marco said confidently.

While Marco was looking around, he was attracted to a yellow spacejet plane; he wanted to take it, but the pilot arrived. The pilot was Lisa.

Lisa said while patting Marco's shoulder and startling him, "Welcome back, sir; I'm sure you don't want to touch my plane, right?"

Lisa was dressed ready for combat, with a painted skull on her face like Nora.

"Oh, no, of course not. I will look for another. But who told you about Calaveras or painted skulls on you?" Marco said, knowing that he only told Nora about the death festival.

She did not respond to the question. "For your safety," Lisa said, "You are required to be my co-pilot."

"What? Only us? Going there? But why?" Marco asked.

Lisa said, "Stop giving double-barreled questions. By the decision of the Apen colonies delegation ministries, to prevent various unwanted things. I must take you to that place myself."

They gave Marco a Nutrition injection that morning. Along with boost for Lisa, they wore the pilot helmet and strong armor. At the front of the runway, the big door opened, and the foundation became open to the outer world.

Marco and Lisa entered together in the yellow plane. Marco asked, "So what's the plan?"

A big bodied robot enters; he is Gustave but unknown to Marco. He said to them, "The plan, Mr. Marco, is straightforward; find and meet the prince on the mountain."

"Change of plan? What if he won't allow it?" Marco asked.

"He will, he will," Gustave said.

Then Marco and Lisa flew out with some other spacejets. Alexa started to fly her plane, but Gustave forbade it.

Gustave said to Alexa, "Captain, you are staying for a while here; we will enter the second wave."

Alexa was confused because they had not been told anything about the plan of attack, but she still followed the protocol.

When Lisa had gotten Marco into the sky, she said, "Look, sir, the mountain is clearly visible in front."

"I can't see anything; the sky is filled with storms," Marco answered.

Lisa said, "Sir, my plane has plenty of sensor devices and artificial map vision; we can see in the fog and clouds. Look at the radar and 3D monitor."

"Oh, right," Marco said.

They flew into the blizzard with bright black clouds. There were about ten southern replica spacejet alliances that followed them, but a heavy snowstrom and wind was powerful—the turbulence made their aircraft shake violently.

"Uhm, my pilot. This doesn't look good," Marco said worriedly.

"Take it easy, sir. Welcome to the New Alps. I call it the Frost-punk," Lisa answered.

Marco looked at the radar. Due to the darkness, he saw one-by-one the aircraft that followed them were lost in the storm.

"Ah, Lisa . . . I have bad news," Marco said after seeing the radar.

Lisa answered again. She said, "Yes sir, I also know; please remain calm."

Suddenly a southern replica plane approached; the pilot said, "Retreat! Back off! I will surrender, we must retreat, captain!" But the flight was then hit by a mighty thunderbolt and it was destroyed beside Lisa's plane.

"OUCH! We will die, Lisa, I'VE EXPERIENCED THIS BEFORE!" Marco shouted nervously.

Lisa remained focused on flying forward into the thick clouds without turning and continued to advance, she seems doesn't are about being killed later. They passed through the turbulence that was getting stronger, and lightning hit close to the side continuously, the light so bright that it could even blind the eyes. But Lisa continued to fly steadily, without retreating. Then all the planes that were with them were lost in a cloud without a trace on the radar.

Seeing the situation, Marco said while holding Lisa's shoulder: "I know this, the same as the attack on my crew — this is from Phoenix; we will not survive; lower your plane!"

Lisa said, "OK."

She then flew her plane low, but the sky was still filled with clouds; only the high mountains were visible in front. Lisa flew in through the holes in the mountain, her plane swirled quickly past the twists and turns of the hills, dodging the lightning strikes. Marco just stayed in the back seat, saying nothing. Then it appeared that the area between the mountains was filled with electricity and plasma.

"WHAT!? There can't be this big whirlwind in the mountains," Marco said because he didn't believe his eyes.

Lisa replied, "What is impossible, sir? Everything is possible in this universe."

"Okay," Marco said, "but I don't want to die first! We are alone here. Where are the others?"

Seeing Marco scared, Lisa said, "Take it easy, sir. There will be a second life; keep your brain intact—we can make you a replica."

Marco took a breath, and said irritably "Second Life? You sounds like Nora. No, the replica is only an AI that copies the dead brain, it's soulless. I still die." Seeing Lisa's face turn sad, Marco said again, "Oh, I'm sorry; I didn't mean to offend you. I mean . . . you are still a human, aren't you? But in AI memory."

"It's okay, sir," said Lisa. "It makes no difference; what you say is right."

They could see the highest mountain on the planet, a mountain that was covered with thick snow. The trip was then smoother than they had thought all this time

Marco said, "I understand now why this planet is called Apen; it comes from the word Alpine. This place resembles the Alps; is this country called New Switzerland?"

"Terraformed for a hundred years, this place was the first colony on this planet," Lisa said.

Marco asked again. "Then, why did they make a colony in this bad place? This is not even calm like the others."

Lisa said "Right, sir, all of this planet was like the Alps at first, but the mountains were flattened into valleys for the construction of the city. Sadly, all that remains are bones; all the hard work of humans just vanished and will be forgotten. Human lives are only as short as death."

Then Marco looked at Lisa's face and whispered in a low voice, "There are the painting of Calaveras or Skulls on your face; I only told Nora once about the Day of the Dead festival. I'm curious how you know this; are you friends?"

"I don't know, sir," replied Lisa. "I don't understand what you are talking about, it's just paint on me. It could be a demon or something—it makes no difference. I don't believe that ghosts are from fallen humans—they're from Fallen Angels to make fun of us."

Suddenly a large door opened from the mountain, like an airstrip in the same ground at Rozenland. Amid of snow, the gate opened wide—a large metal door descended, making visible a large airfield inside. Lisa directed her plane to land there. There were also many large crystals formed through electricity, like hills of glowing transparent crystals containing plasma substances. Their plane landed in a safe place on the runway.

"This place looks insecure," Marco said after jumping down from his plane.

Lisa said, "Sir, you have been equipped with much safety equipment and many tools; go ahead."

"Where do I go?" Marco asked.

"Meet the prince; he must be in this building," replied Lisa.

"You're not coming?" Marco asked again.

"No, sir, the task of the southern forces is only to take you in." Lisa shook her head as if she was not participating.

By steeling himself, Marco began to walk in. The military headquarters there seemed dead—there was no electricity or anyone else.

No electricity? Then how can the anvil gate be opened? He thought.

Lisa just stood near her plane on the runway, while Marco continued to move forward. Like a clueless person, he wasn't sure what to do anymore, all of his efforts will be ended close to the goal. He just wanted to end everything.

Alexa then called," Monsieur Marco, are you in?"

"Yes, now what?" He answered while questioning..

"Go in, look for the prince. He really wants to meet you," Alexa replied.

Gustave, who was next to Alexa, said secretly to her, "Captain Alexa, tell him to secure the white capsules and black capsules. He have to leave quickly, no need to meet the prince."

Alexa then called Marco and said, "Sir, there is something you have to do; look for capsules . . . " Suddenly his voice was cut off.

A magnetic wave came out, destroying all electronic items on Marco's body, including cameras, sheets, phones and more. Shocked at that, Marco had fallen, but he was fine and tried to get up again.

* * *

Prince? Who the hell is he? It's troublesome; how about how to kill him with a deadly weapon, Marco thought.

He looked back, an energy shield had blocked the way, preventing him from returning; he now had no choice—he had to move forward. Feeling curious and worried, he ventured on to face an uncertain fate. Between chaos and storms, someone who is cornered must be able to act. As he continued walking, he looked forward, and there was a location that was very brightly lit. Like a cave in the middle of a crystal mountain in the edge of the dead runway. Marco looked at the prince, who was sitting on a throne made of light blue-white crystals. Marco just silently watched the man seated, in pale, fancy prince's clothes, his eyes glowing like lightning and his skin vibrant like electricity. The man infused with dragon power.

The prince said with a human voice mixed with thunder, "I am Michael, the only human left over the explosion of plasma waves a century ago. The Universe is formed not only from energy and matter but also a force, which maintains a balance between heavenly bodies. This Universe is vast, but many things are bigger than the universe itself, but that knowledge is no use to you; how to defeat the Fallen Angels is the most important for you. I accidentally sacrificed my entire planet, but no, they did it, not me. Their research destroyed everything I love; everyone died to save our galaxy from destruction by getting this much knowledge. I got the weapon from our enemy the Dragon, and another Fallen Angel monster named Abaddon. To defeat the zeal light, you need magnate force, just as light energy cannot get out of the power of a black hole. Dragon wants to destroy all life in a cursed universe, then attack the other Fallen Angels so that only they are left—so that the universe becomes clean of sin. But what about their sin? They also planned to destroy the stars of their homes that would kill them, then achieve their dreams to clear the universe of chaos, silence, and death. They hope that when the wages of sin which are death can be paid, the Dimensional Kingdom will forgive them. But that's foolishness."

Marco said "Is it true that you are a half-dragon human, who with your power has killed the entire planet?"

The prince said again, "They did it, not me, I'm just a survivor. I tried to stop them in the researching state, but the power was too big to learn; they accidentally sacrificed my own planet for the safety of the entire galaxy. That brought sadness to my heart for the rest of my life. I have both of these weapons stored here, one made from the power of the energy of the Dragon who lives in the living star and another force from the Abaddon who lives in the death star. You take it and make your decision."

I think I have to play the game, Marco thought.

The prince then pointed at two one-meter capsules close by, lying on the floor. One was blue, and the other was almost transparent.

Marco said, "No, you take it yourself."

"Listen to me, son, I can't touch it," the Prince said, "It will explode. I don't know what will happen after that—it probably will kill me and the entire planet."

Marco took the two objects, then asked, "Who are you . . . really?"

The Prince replied "I can feel from your vein that there is my blood flowing there, also—from my daughter, Jasmin. I have save you from the radiation all this time from afar with my power."

"Radiation? Jasmin?" Marco said in surprise, "Wait, she is my grandmother! So I'm your great grandson? Grandma died a long time ago; my parents also died in an accident. Is that why they were very paranoid and often hid?"

The Prince said, "They sacrificed millions of soldiers to entering this surface for a century; Phoenix will never let anyone in nor out, but I will help my own blood no matter what they want. Ten years ago, Phoenix killed millions of space people. Only one survived—named Lee—but he later died. Nevertheless, information about the capsule arrived at space people. They then trapped you here. "

Marco was annoyed. He ventured to say, "Trapped, you said? Yeah, i know. But that capsules, this thing killed my friends and the whole planet. Are you thirsty for strength and will now give this to me? No, I'm not interested in being a murderer!"

CHAPTER 18

Marco angrily shot the capsules, trying to destroy them.

The Prince then stood up from his chair and walked towards Marco while saying, "My child, you cannot destroy them. Forgive me even though you don't want to, I can't control them, my son. I have never asked for this power, but I must be grateful. Phoenix and Dragon are out of my control. I just hide here, feeling sorry and regret for many, long years. Their research on the weapon has killed many people; accidentally, the fact that I'm the only one alive with this form is a miracle. Now everything is in your possession; I will no longer be bound by dead, and it is enough for me."

All of a sudden, an explosion occurred. A dangerous force-powered bomb had been installed in Marco's body while he was sleeping. He had been tricked by Ariana at the time in Nova Anglia after being drugged and operated on by Central. The explosion left Marco dead and he lost his stomach completely. The power of the bomb touched the Prince, but he did not fall, but instead made unstable Dragon energy around the place. The signal on Marco's body turned back on and told everyone that the capsules were indeed there.

"Look at the sky!" Gustave said to Alexa, "Marco has defeated the prince! The power of Phoenix has weakened in the air—their energy-saving crystals have been broken!"

"How is that possible? Really?" Alexa said after knowing that they had installed a powerful, layered bomb in Marco's body.

With the voice of a spirited robot, Gustave ordered, "Send the sign of my troops! Let the space forces find out. Phoenix has been weakened; let's attack and grab the weapon!"

They were then able to quickly send a message into space, before the Phoenix power recovered. Ariana, who was in charge of monitoring the Apen star system, received it, and sent the fleet from the nearest Galactic League from UW, GaiGa, and Central.

The UW then sent troops quickly; the closest human colonies then formed an emergency council to send their admiral to the location.

An earth council in the distant star system then drew up forces; someone said at an emergency meeting, "All the nearby colonies of the Apen star system have reported loyalty to United Worlds and Watcher of GaiGa. The following is a list of military alliances participating in the first wave of attacks along with the colonies of their original planet:

1. The Kingdoms of Commonwealth armada from the Nova Anglia Colonies.
2. The European Lineage armada of the French Vasileon Knight Colony, Germanic Mega Fort, and the Eve Viking Colony.
3. The Slavic Blood armada from the Stanislav Mining Colony, Pavlov Dominion, and the great Unidova.
4. The Pacific Unity armada from the same system, which is the New Molucca Colony from Planet Nusa, and Garden Colonies from Planet Nui Nusa or Big Nusa.
5. And the Latin Order armada of the Romanium the Fifth Colony.

This alliance armada will come with the strength of five hundred million military manpower, not counting humanoid robots and family members of the crew.

Following is the list of Fleets from nearby colonies which still delay but approve attacks in the second stage: African Union, Orient Dynasty, Southeast Association, Sinai Ring, Southern Nations, Centric Bloc, and United of America. Any change in this form will be delivered as soon as possible."

After the council meeting, troops were flown to the Apen planet from their separate worlds. Not inferior to the human fleet, other Galactic League fleets such as Central sent nearly one billion androids, and the GaiGa Clan sent five billion Felidean through the Watcher board, but it would take them longer to get there because of the location of their colonies far from humans. The human fleet was from the Galactic League faction which, until the very beginning, came to collect the two capsules that were known to still exist. This wasn't the most massive operation ever created, but, indeed, it was one of the largest ones.

* * *

Meanwhile on the planet Apen, two years had passed since that incident; the entire main fleet of the first wave of the five UW sub-factions alliance had gathered and arrived with two Central squadrons. They have sent spies to attack the Dragon there. After all this time, according to the spies, they found out the prince's current position was not far from his first position. Alexa was assigned to be sent there, too, along with several Central robots that arrived, led by an android named Ariana. Alexa landed on the same foundation, and she found an android — Lisa's replica body — still fell on the floor; after losing her location for years, they finally found her in those deadly mountains. Ariana was called and then came with an energy device and tried to wake Lisa; it worked. Feeling shocked, as if she had just risen, Lisa opened her eyes and immediately stood,

181

looking at her surroundings. Lisa looked at them with sharp eyes.

Ariana said, "Calm, Miss Replica, we are here to help."

Lisa then ran from them without saying anything.

"Follow her," ordered Ariana to several members.

After all this time, Alexa also did not know the real incident because it was still hidden by Gustave and Ariana that Marco had been trapped. She then returned to bring his spacejet to patrol. Many UW camps had been installed on the land and mountains. But they were only filled by remote-controlled Droid soldiers by human operators from far space who use the mind controller in sleeping tubes on the Motherships. UW and Central have also bombarded the remnants of STARS from the planet and cleaned up the rebellious Wonderland. The others kept trying to dig through the place, looking for the presence of the prince who was hiding.

Lisa ran hard looking for Marco around the mountain basement but did not find him. Suddenly some Androids who followed her from behind were electrocuted and killed. Lisa was amazed to see that; then from the front, she saw a large Mecha standing up, Mecha is a Dutchman.

The Dutchman said, "Follow me, miss."

Without hesitation, Lisa followed him, and found Nora in a hidden room, sitting there without her left hand. Lisa and Nora had known each other long before the incident.

Lisa said "I failed to protect Marco, Nora. He was killed; they put a bomb on his body without our knowledge."

"You mean him?" answered Nora, pointing to a crystal.

There was Marco's body in the crystal—still intact.

"How is that possible?" Lisa said in surprise.

Nora said, "Dear. The prince is his great grandfather, he saved Marco by giving him some small power of Dragon; he will recover soon. It turned out that the explosion came from a research center in this place which was funded and managed by the Galactic League. Prince Michael didn't created it, but it destroyed our planet. Prince only hid himself feeling sorry for him all these years; Dragon become alive and uncontrolled, while outsiders wanted to get the dangerous weapon. We can't let them have it."

Suddenly Ariana and Gustave appeared behind them.

Ariana said, "Girls, tell us. Where is the capsule located?"

"Oh, it is here; brash robots deliberately sent people who knew nothing about this planet just to die for their experiments," Nora said.

"Calm down, ladies," Gustave said. "We do this for the good of everyone; the capsule contains weapons that can be very dangerous if they fall into the wrong hands."

"Dutchman don't give it to them," Nora said.

"Alright, lady! I will take care of it until . . ." Suddenly, there was a loud explosion and Dutchman was shot by Gustave before finishing his words. He fell motionless, spilling oil everywhere from his body.

Lisa and Nora were shocked to see the incident but stood there sadly.

Gustave, with his big new body, advanced to surround them and said, "Listen to me carefully. Don't let all the sacrifices of the robots and humans go to waste. Give up the capsule!"

"Forget it," Ariana said, and she took the capsule from the dead body of Dutchman. "Where is the other one?" Asked Ariana.

Nora just kept quiet. Ariana approached her angrily and shouted, "WHERE'S THE OTHER ONE, YOU CURSED REPLICAN?!"

"You only need to ask him politely," Nora answered.

"To him? OK, who?" Asked Ariana then looked at Marco who was still frozen in the crystal. Ariana said, "Gustave, finish your mission — destroy the crystal."

Gustave became stiff, and after he stood still for a moment, Ariana became angry again. Finally, Gustave advanced to brace himself and destroy the crystal with a punch. Marco's body then fell to the floor.

"Hah, it's effortless," Gustave said.

When Gustave was about to lift Marco, he found another capsule there. Suddenly, Marco opened his eyes. He recognized Gustave's voice, and then hit him, the big Gustave slamming against the wall.

"What is this, why am I strong?" Marco said then looked at Ariana and said, "You! You sent us to die on this planet. Why didn't you tell me first? Why were my friends brought in?"

Ariana said, "Tell you, sir? You can run away or even join Dragon like this now. Yes, we can just wash your brain to obey, but come on . . . where is the fun in that? Prince are powerful enough to know people's mind. I have been managing experiments on this planet all this time. This is very exciting. By the way, your stupid boss, Franky, indirectly the ones who help me, I managed to plant the bomb on your stomach, while you were sleeping after the party."

Ariana's response anger Marco and he struck back; an energy shot came out of his hand. Marco was very shocked and said, "Wow, what is this?! I have great strength?"

The electricity was visible from his hand; Marco became excited. After being the weakest on the planet for so long, running around to avoid many things, finally he could help his friends, and they were the ones who needed to be saved.

Gustave laughed from afar and said, "Ha ha ha ha! That! There it is—the power that many people pursue. Imagine what we can do with it!"

Marco continued to shoot Ariana with bursts of electricity that somehow came out of his hand. Marco felt weak like he was hungry after each shot. When he stopped, he saw that Ariana, with her advanced android body, had absorbed all of that energy, and became stronger and quickly shot back with her palm, emitting a laser beam. Marco was injured because of that. Nora then took out an automatic revolver gun containing a hundred projectiles in one bullet—like a Gatling gun—and shot Ariana; Lisa took Marco away.

Ariana then chased Lisa who had Marco and the two capsules, leaving Nora, with her one hand, to fight the big Gustave.

Gustave said, "Forgive us about your city, Wonderland made a bad decision, so we had to respond from our side. Constantine has betrayed me; he must die."

Gustave and Nora then fought each other. Lisa brought the capsules with Marco; they had to get out of Ariana's high-speed pursuit.

"My strength has recovered! Put me down. Take the capsule away!" Marco said, then descended and blocked Ariana.

Marco said, "You! Looks like you have to die!"

"Get away, you are Dragon! You are corrupt and monstrous," Ariana said in an aggressive tone.

Flying craft noises began to sound; UW and Central spaceships had approached the mountains.

Ariana said, "Listen, sir? That is the sound of your death; you will be a good subject for us. Come on, it's for the benefit of mankind, isn't it?"

Angry, Marco said, "Monica . . . oh, not those, but Hendrik and other friends. What about their benefit? Do you care?"

Ariana just laughed and said, "People die every second, from trillions of humanity and Androids; losing some groups for the benefit of everyone is heroic. They will be remembered, like you, pity man."

"Remembered?" Marco said, "You fooled them! The entire planet has died from the research of Dragon's and Abaddon's weapons—your research. Will you do the same thing in another place?"

"Oh, you're just wasting my time!" Ariana said, then shot Marco.

He dodged and was about to shoot back, but was afraid that his energy shots would only make Ariana stronger. Ariana then left Marco there and went looking for Lisa, who still holding the capsule. Marco followed them. There were a lot of camps and military posts as well as UW exploration droids everywhere. The posts were controlled by Droid forces and guided by human operators from far away in the sky; they marked the location between those who could enter and those who were quarantined because there were Dragon Crystals. Lisa ran towards her yellow spacejet which had been on the runway for two years.

* * *

Ariana gave the command to the UW patrol aircraft in the sky. "Reporting in, Marco is still alive, and the capsule is still in their group. Send help immediately."

"Understood; the pilot will immediately head to you," answered an operator at the space station.

UW then sent planes and drones to chase Marco's group. Droids fell there, and the latest Cerberus drones were deployed. When Marco's team was cornered, something happened. The amount of movement on the mountain awoke the Dragon monsters who were still sleeping.

Marco looked at them and said, "Come on, great grandfather. Do something; I know you're still hiding, but don't let your mistakes be repeated. Let's act!"

Ariana, who was running, realized Marco was behind her when she heard his words. A large flash descended from the sky and struck one of the areas there—the area that was being quarantined by UW, Dragon's sleeping crystals. That angered the monsters, so a lot of Phoenix and Monsters came out that had never been seen before.

The lands trembled, and there were landslides everywhere. A UW droid soldier said, "Look! There are movements from all directions—everything is ready on the spot!"

Black clouds appeared on the ground, then lightning came; the weather darkened from what had been a bright day, leaving everything pitch black. Out of the darkness, blue lights glowed and sparkled from a distance. The UW droid army monitored the events from afar. Various mysterious creatures mixed with energy emerged; the monsters were shaped from animals to humans that emitted blue light from their half-corpse bodies. The horror monsters made by the Dragon advanced as fast as sound and were not seen attacking all the Droids there. Some planes and Copper tried to avoid them, but there were some Monsters that could jump and catch them in the air.

"Post fifteen reporting to the command center; we are attacked by energy monsters. Please send extra droid help; they are faster than our bullets!"

The Droids and their posts were torn apart, with bursts of terrible fire and crystal swords coming out of their bodies. Like in smoke and lightning, that's how they walk—creatures that were once good now have become corrupt because of Dragon's power.

From a distance, splashes and horrible screams between the sounds of gunfire rang out to Marco. He asked himself, "What is that sound? What creature is that?"

"Transgon, they became more powerful with dragon's energy," Nora said from behind, startling him. "They were once strong forces of the countries around the New Alpen Mountains in the southernmost region—the Reisläufer forces that have been possessed, the undead Swiss Knight corpses, buried beneath the snows, now raise again."

"Wait," Marco said. "Where is Gustave?"

"OOPS, LOOK BEHIND YOU!" Nora shouted.

Suddenly Gustave appeared with an angry voice, his eyes glowing red. He had been shot by Nora.

"Hey! Dwarf. Where are you going to hide after you run out of bullets? Super-grandpa won't be able to save your ass this time!" Gustave growled, pointing at them.

Gustave then opened his chest and shot energy quickly towards them. Nora used her android body to protect Marco, which caused her to burn because of the energy shots.

"OH NO! YOU'RE BURNING, NORA!" Marco shouted frantically.

Gustave then grabbed Nora, pulling her until she fell into the bottom ravine between the snows.

"Sorry sir, I have to do this!" Gustave said, opening his chest again to shoot.

Marco quickly released the electrical energy in his hand and shot Gustave's chest, causing severe damage to Gustave. The robot then walked backward while beginning to burn.

Alexa called Gustave and said, "Hello, Colonel, say what happened? Is Marco still alive?"

"Yes! He has been powered by Dragon! He is a devil, kill him, captain!" Gustave said to Alexa while burning.

Marco was about to take his energy out of his hand again to shoot Gustave, but the heat did not come out. Marco felt a powerful feeling of hunger in his stomach.

Marco thought, *Hungry; does this energy only need food for replenish? I'm in luck!*

He saw one of the Transgon creatures armored in heavy metal—a white knight with a long lightning sword, and ghostly sharp-eyed. While filled with the electricity of Dragon's power that Michael gave, he ran fast to avoid them, looking again at the direction of the Droid camps, hoping that there was food there. Marco then quickly jumped and ran faster than he had ever run; it hurt his legs a bit. After arriving at the camps, he found that everything there was just a machine.

Controlled Droid? Of course; UW won't repeat the same mistakes, they don't want to lose human lives anymore, or perhaps this place are extremely radiated, he thought.

CHAPTER 19

Not finding anything other than battery and equipment tools carried by the droids, Marco was about to go back to look for Nora but decided that Lisa's condition was more critical, so he went towards Ariana. As he left, Transgon monsters came near Marco and attacked him.

He dodged quickly, "Almost!" he said.

Transgon looked at Marco as an enemy just like the Prince, even though they had almost the same strength source.

"Dutchman, yes, I have to jump like that poor man," as he said when he saw the headquarters on the snow mountain to run away from Transgon.

He then jumped very high with the help of energy he got from Prince, but when he landed, his leg was broken.

Painfully, Marco saw the blood coming out. He said, "Ouch, Oh crap, my legs! That was stupid. It seems that I watch too many superheroes movies."

He then saw Lisa being surrounded by Android forces with Ariana there, near Lisa's yellow plane. Marco saw the Chasseur plane, which was the plane Alexa was using, and the Chasseur plane flew towards their position.

"NO, DON'T APPROACH HER! The weapon is too dangerous for you; stop!" Marco shouted, but because of the strong wind and long distance, he was not heard.

Marco then shot them with a focus on his hands; after a few seconds came the light of energy that arrived at one of the

Central androids near Ariana. Some of them turned and flew towards Marco while the others were still near Lisa, surrounding her and forcing her to give them both capsules.

Then Ariana said to Lisa, "It's a pity; the second life you use against mankind. Don't waste any more time—give it up, or I will shoot."

Marco was surrounded, too, then he saw a Chasseur plane that was about to come close; he felt hopeless because his leg was broken. The unexpected happened; the Chasseur began to shoot at the android central forces which surrounded them. They fall apart, and not a single bullet hit Marco or Lisa.

Ariana, who was injured said via radio, "Ariana here reporting. A replica defected again; it seems we can't trust them anymore. Anyone, shoot that stupid Chasseur spacejet!"

A droid colonel called back and said, "UW droids are here; we are overwhelmed by monsters! We cannot help anyone—or even ourselves. How pathetic."

The droids were then slowly destroyed along with their excavation camps. After two years of hard work, the first recorded troops were almost exhausted. UW from the sky saw that the admirals of the five factions began to negotiate. They started to land all of their droids; already, there were around twenty million deployed below.

Robot troops, robotic forces; it seems like I'm still the only human here, Marco thought after seeing drop pod and parachutes that filled the sky float down to the ground, like an iron rain from the clouds.

Someone came near Marco; she was Nora with a hot body and only one arm. Nora said "Look at that, darling, a snowfall; black snow from metal was seen emerging from the sky."

Alexa saw that then flew back, but she was followed by many of Freddy's planes from Wonderland led by General Boneheart, a successor to Constantine. Boneheart came with a mask of a lion skull on his head and Axe on his back.

Marco said, "Look, everyone is gathering from all directions; this is crazy."

Nora looked at Boneheart's plane from the ground and said "Look; that Klossmajor is coming again."

Boneheart said through a voice channel that was hacked to Alexa. "Drittsekker, bite i gresset! A sad day in my mind; when will you learn, how many must be killed? I will bring that death to you for your actions. Out of my way, you dogs! Robots have no sin; I have no sins to confess."

Alexa didn't answer. Boneheart with a jet named Thor flew like lightning, neared Alexa's Chasseur and then tried to shoot her with exploding electric fire. From air to ground; shots, explosions, and troops that killed—all of the events of the day brought something worse.

Nora took Marco away from there, while Lisa took the plane. Ariana lost both legs because she was shot by Alexa's Chasseur. When Lisa was about to fly away to carry the two capsules, Ariana suddenly flew to hold Lisa's yellow plane wing.

"WAIT, DWARF! Our business isn't done yet, and YOU, TOO, SIR!" Gustave's screaming voice came from behind Marco and Nora.

Gustave, who was still burning in the chest, ran to strangle Nora and Marco with his hands. Nora used her gun and shot Gustave's hands until he released them.

"Oh, oh . . . this is bad," Gustave said.

Without his injured hands, Gustave ran backward, but he still insisted on attacking; at first he wanted to hold them and then shot them with his stomach energy, but now he was using his palm barrel.

Suddenly Prince appeared like an electric explosion in front of Marco; the prince's hand touched Gustave's mouth and made him explode, shattering into metal ash.

Nora, who was nearby said "That was great; Like Zeus and

Thor, he came. You must be responsible for completing this, prince! Finish what you started!"

The prince said in a thunderous voice, "The Dragons will move further, find a place to shelter, and find a place to destroy another colony."

"What? We can't let that happen!" Marco said in surprise while still lying on the floor because of his broken legs.

Then there was a strong earthquake from afar, so high that the mountain moved, but the quake did not expand. An abundant light appeared, and then emitted plasma waves.

"Plasma waves! Oh, no, I will die again," said Nora.

But these waves were different; the rush of energy passed through the UW droid camps and transformed them into the eyeless and empty mouth like Transgon, but their eye holes emitted terrible blue light. Droid robots, their AI-controlled planes changed direction, now attacking their creators.

The wave reached replicas like Lisa, Alexa, and Nora but miraculously they were not affected. Marco was surprised to see his friends unaffected. He saw the Prince, and the prince smiled.

"You know my friends, thank you, but forget it; I still hate you, too," Marco said.

"Listen to me," said Prince. "I can't control them, but only lure them out. I must destroy the Dragon, as I should have done a hundred years ago. Dragon will target you and me because we have succeeded in using their power independently."

"Who are they? Central and UW or Dragon? Or Star Ranger?" Marco asked.

The prince answered, "Everybody; everyone from humans to dark angels. The Universe consists of visible and invisible codes, created by the Creators of the Dimensional Kingdom. I accidentally broke the universe code which made Dragon angry, and they came to surround me all along. The Realm is made of three worlds: the world that we live in is the universe; the underworld is the world without worlds; and the Heaven as the world nobody will ever understand."

"Oh, that's too complicated! Simplify it!" Marco said.

Nora, who was near them, said, "Like our computer system? The software as the world, hardware as the underworld, and operator room above as the heaven — but in things that are more mysterious and impossible to understand. So the Dragon and the Abaddon who were fallen angels are the moderators who got kicked out by admin; how funny is that."

The prince said, "Yes, but all of this realm is created by the Dimensional Kingdom; the fallen have more opportunities and strength than ordinary beings like us. Enough. Listen, you are the hope of the galaxy our World; we will save them, but they will hate us. Time is running out; I will leave." The prince rose to the sky; slowly his body turned into blue lightning and expanded into a giant.

In the sky Boneheart's plane was no longer visible to Alexa; quickly, Boneheart's plane lit up like lightning because it was infected with Transgon. Then the flight fired thunder shots that chased Alexa's plane, the Chasseur crashing down near the runway.

* * *

Knowing that Alexa had been destroyed along with her plane, Marco remembered Monica who had been gone a long time, and was sad. Nora saw that and ran to where the plane had fallen. Confused and alone, but not giving up, Marco crawled in search of a flight that could be ridden at a military airport that had been abandoned for a hundred years.

"Hopefully, this will work," Marco said as he crawled up on a fighter jet; even though his legs were broken, with difficulty he successfully climbed into the pilot's seat.

A spark in his hand made the plane glow miraculously; the frozen sheets suddenly functioned, the aircraft's energy battery alive again. Marco then ascended into the sky, looking for Lisa; a stream that could not appear, as a signal line of different dimensions, appeared in his eyes. He knew Lisa's position and flew towards her.

"Oh, no. But good! This is not just ordinary energy, but a universal codes that I control—this is amazing." Marco said to himself while looking forward.

Remote control planes with AI from UW and Central who were possessed with Transgon went crazy and attacked any flying craft crews that were still conscious. Droids below then shot back planes and other droid troops were about to go down. While Lisa was flying nearby, she saw from a window a central robot; the robot was Ariana, but she looked different. Ariana had become Transgon, her eyes were blue like ghosts, and from her body, and blue smoke like fire came out. Marco approached trying to help Lisa escape.

Marco approached and made a swirling hand gesture as a code for Lisa.

"Good," Lisa answered, then she twirled her plane until Ariana was released, detached from her wings.

From behind, Marco shot Ariana until she was destroyed.

Marco shouted, "YES! VERY SATISFIED!" Marco said, "The bastard is dead; too bad he died in a trance, but the important thing is the robot died."

There were many planes behind them, some manned and some who weren't. Some human pilots started flying. Many AI pilots became Transgon, so fleshy pilots began to operate. But the human patrol pilots touched Dragon's palm wave and turned into Transgons. Two groups, from Transgon and those who were aware, chased Lisa's plane.

He tried calling for help from his replica friends at

Rozenland. He said, "Emergency. I need your help!" But no one answered; it seemed like they had been possessed with Transgon.

He then saw the Prince, revealing himself as a two-hundred meters great energy form.

Marco, who was flying in the air, thought, *Come on, great grandfather; show that you are really on our side.*

The prince then tried to throw a lightning spear from his hand towards the planes that were approaching Marco and Lisa. The lightning spear was vast and destroyed everything in front of it. A spaceship appeared from the sky; the ship was a hundred and fifty-meter Destroyer-type but had become Transgon. From inside the ship, there was a battle between the crew who had turned into monsters and those who were still alive. The Prince then made a decision—he made a new lightning spear and threw it on the ship. It took two times before the ship split into two. That made the other Transgon monsters angry, and from the mountains there appeared many Transgon monsters who were poised to jump and fly towards the Prince, he made another spear and turned it to hit the hills.

Then from the place of the quake, a massive explosion appeared like a spectacular volcano, but it was no longer the plasma wave that came out, but a giant Dragon which was reddish blue, which was formed from pure-energy. The weather suddenly brightened, and the Dragon gushed a breath of fire on the Prince that broke him.

Corrupted Seraphim, Marco thought. *Oh, no, my great grandfather has disappeared.*

Lisa flew toward Marco. He saw her while raising her hand's gesture to ask. Marco didn't know what to do to defeat the Dragon.

Lisa flew over and booked the plane's glass; she said with a loudspeaker, "Do you have a plan, sir? I mean, Marco."

Marco shouted, "Whatever happens, DON'T LET ANYONE GET THE CAPSULE! That will only bring death like this planet!"

"Death?" Lisa replied. "I won't let them get it, and regarding that death, I'll take care of it."

Marco just looked confused and said, "Whatever; good luck. Let's think of a way out together; I will look for others."

"Yes," Lisa said. "Look for Nora; she is still down there somewhere. Find her and get away from here."

"Be careful," Marco said, flying his plane away from her.

"DANKE MARCO." Lisa shouted from afar, and then said "Vielen Dank. Good bye," in calmed voice.

In a hurry, Marco flew in search of Nora at the crash site of Alexa.

All eyes looked at an extraordinary astral Dragon that growing bigger and bigger in the sky. It was clearly glowing as if to run from the planet.

* * *

Spaceships from the Galactic League—UW, Central, and GaiGa—shot the Dragon. Something unexpected appeared; the Star Ranger space fleet appeared out of nowhere, undetected on their radar.

An admiral said to the others, "Look, Star Ranger is here. How could it be?"

The other Admiral replied, "When Phoenix weakens in the atmosphere, STARS must send a signal to their base just like us."

"It's messy, messy; I like this," said the other Admiral named Rasputin. "So? We have to annihilate the Dragon, defeat the Star Rangers while looking for capsules which are the ultimate weapons? Very nice. All right, starboys, shoot to kill."

They then divided the task, one admiral looking for capsules, two against Dragon and the other two against Star Ranger. But their plans fall apart when the spaceships they think are friends have turned into Transgon and attacked everyone. Armed Central and GaiGa were also there and intervened to help their troubled friends.

When the spacejet troops came out, they said "Bullets from every direction! This is crazy! We don't know who the enemy is and who is not! Please, command center, helps us detect them."

The command center answered, "We received your request; we have marked every plane that is hostile in red on your screen. Continue the operation."

The Spacejet group was named Wingman, and they were the most famous pilots among UW forces. Losing a lot of droids forced people to intervene by flying their vehicles with their own hands. The dragon flew into many spaceships and severely damaged them; some of their engines even fought them. Many pilots were increasingly possessed and went crazy. The dragon was about to fly to another colony. Before it became stronger due to starlight, they had to be able to stop the Dragon.

An Admiral from Slavic Blood army ordered spaceships that were still under his command to form a line of walls in the space. They shot the Dragon with special weapons created to make the Dragon overheat, but their energy weapons consumed too much energy.

The Admiral—named Rasputin—said to the Commonwealth Admiral named James Jaydan by communication device, "Admiral James, please bring your troops from behind so we can trap this slut Dragon!"

Admiral James replied, "Good, Admiral, but, what about you? The dragon continues to advance."

"Hah! I will survive!" Admiral Rasputin replied.

James acted immediately, and sent his ships to attack the Dragon from behind, but the Dragon flew and grew and then crashed into many of Rasputin's crafts; his tail hit and made many of James's ship engines jam.

From the other direction, the Latin Fleet and Pacific Fleet were busy attacking Star Ranger, assisted by many spaceships from GaiGa using their favorite long-range spaceship called Monitor.

The Fleet was led by Admiral Philip Bonavento and Admiral Mela Amiri, while GaiGa was led by two Felidean named FerXin and ExAti. They tried to block the Star Ranger fleet that tried to get inside the planet.

Central was led by their Android, while the ES Fleet was led by Admiral Bernard Jagger, a German-polish guy who tried to find the capsules; they all chased after Lisa and Marco. From inside the planet, millions of broad planes and ships flew towards the clouds, like a new layer of the sky coming down, hiding the ground with their blades.

* * *

Marco landed to get Nora, sitting between the destroyed Alexa's plane.

Marco said from inside the plane, "Nora, it's just us; let's get out of here. We can save our sadness for later."

"Good, Marco," Nora answered languidly, then got on Marco's plane, but a shot fell from above, smashing Marco's tail; Nora pulled Marco out of the plane.

"Our plane is destroyed! What do we do now?" Marco asked in pain.

Nora said, "Look, Marco, he is Boneheart! He has become Transgon! Ah, it makes no difference; it's just the same behavior."

"What weapon do you have?" Marco asked.

"Only this revolver," replied Nora.

Marco then held the gun with Nora and lifted it to the sky. He drained the weapon with energy, then together they aimed it at the Boneheart plane that glowed like lightning. Boneheart circled his plane and was about to attack Marco for his final shot.

"Where is Lisa?" asked Nora.

Marco answered, "We will meet her; she waits in the sky . . . and we will get out of here."

"You're stupid; she won't come back," Nora answered.

Marco was shocked hearing that and said, "Wait, isn't she back? Who will she take the capsule? To friends or foes?"

Nora looked at Marco and said, "Sir . . . she will leave forever; when the two capsules are combined, there will be a mass explosion called Nova."

"Are we all going to die?" Marco said in surprise.

"Yes" answered Nora. "Imagine if the weapon fell into the wrong hands, the enemy would steal it from them sooner or later. Then the weapon would spread throughout the galaxy, almost unlimited with great power, killing quickly."

"So that's their goal," Marco said.

Nora hit his head and said, "Ha ha ha, of course. That's everyone's goal. We died, Marco! We won't let anyone experience this again!"

Marco reacted. "Lucky you; you have already died. Those words seem like a relief for you — fine — but they will kill me," Marco said.

"So much history to remain here, forgotten . . . it's sad." She said.

CHAPTER 20

The Boneheart plane was approaching; then, when one of them shot towards the plane, one of its wings was broken, making the plane, containing unstable energy, fall near them. Boneheart fell into the snow and was invisible, thanks to the energy bullets that combine with Marco's power.

"We succeeded!" Marco said, "All right, now we are just waiting for time—this place is going to explode. I am very scared, Nora."

The two then sat near the destroyed Chasseur plane. They had lost a lot of energy, and were unable to stand up anymore.

In space, Lisa flew towards the Dragon carrying the two Nova capsules in her hand.

"The energy capsule and capsule force are in front of everything forward! But hold your shot, we must be able to trap him," said a Wingman to his group.

Behind Lisa, there were many planes gathering after her, reaching the atmosphere and out into space. Then came more large planes and spaceships, all of them following her.

Lisa looked to the side and said "This is the time, the second death."

She was about to commit suicide when she saw the Dragon still far away and continued to fly towards the location fearing that the Nova explosion would not be big enough. The planes that followed her began to enter into battle, Star Ranger ships flew in and Transgon planes started to appear, coming from the direction of Planet and Dragon. The situation became anarchic. Lisa did her best to avoid all of that, as the large ships, measuring five hundred meters to thousands of meters, began to attack each other.

A Wingman said to his captain with enthusiasm, "Sir! Sir! I see her! Soon, the power of the Dragon will be ours!"

"Follow her" replied the Wingman captain.

From the front of the Wingman, appeared Wasp planes from the Ranger. This time they came from a remote star system, and the Wasp looks more powerful, not a corpse. Their armor was the best equipment from biological and robotic that could be made, a perfect flying space Cyborg forces.

Back on the ground, Marco began to fall asleep due to lack of oxygen.

Nora said "Look at that, Marco! The Cerberus drone and the Gendarmerie robot. I haven't seen those who are still perfect for a long time," she said, pointing to Admiral Bernard's troops from the approaching ES fleet. Nora said again "How does it feel to be sick as fleshy creatures? I have long forgotten it."

"Sick? I feels sick of them," Marco answered.

She continued, "It is a curse when all people have free will to do whatever they want; pain is made so that we learn; death, so that our sins will not last long in the universe. The wages of sin is death."

"You could be a good writer, an android one," Marco said.

Nora said again while pointing at sky, "Look, they come, just keep quiet."

A large plane that looked different from the others appeared and landed in front of them. Then a high-ranking person from UW approached; he was a droid controlled by Admiral Bernard from space.

"It seems like the new human will never learn about the true pain and death," Nora said, looking at the UW and Central planes that landed in front of them on the snow hill.

Then the admiral said in a big voice, speaking "Don't move, don't fight; we come for your good."

A large droid looks down, walks up to Marco, and greets him; the admiral said again, "Mr. Marco, humans need you, we need you, come with me."

"Don't!" Nora whispered. "They will put you in their crazy labs, they will study you so they can copy all the power you have for their war."

"I am Admiral Bernard, vowing to protect your rights as a normal human," said the voice from the droid.

Nora whispered again, "Don't listen to him, they don't look at you again as an ordinary person; those are trap words."

"No, leave me alone, I beg you, stop it, how many billions people has to die for this power?" Marco answered the admiral.

"Bist du dir sicher? If you want it rough, then it will be done as you said. It's not just about billions, it's about the entire human species, we need that power," said the biggest Droid who was Admiral Bernard.

Other Droids then surrounded them, drones appeared to guard the sky and other robots prepared to catch and sedate Marco. The number of droids was many on the ground, like black sand on snow around them.

* * *

From the sky on the mothership from the ES fleet of Vasileon Knights, Admiral Bernard who controlled the droids himself monitored the screen. Suddenly his gaze was distracted; the Dragon in the sky began to emit its enormous energy as if the Dragon would fly away quickly to the other colonies. All the worst dreams that can occur, monsters that will devour other lives, billions of lives will be wasted in vain, in unknowingness.

Marco and his friend could not allow that to happen, while other humans only cared for weapons in the capsule, for the sake of their unbroken war.

All the droids on the ground then looked at the sky, because the droid operators witnessed a horrible event from their spaceship. Lisa watched everything from space, then flew as hard as she could towards the Dragon while carrying the capsules.

A Wingman pilot said, "Sir, the replica named Lisa seems to be carrying the capsules towards Dragon!"

His admiral said, "Towards the Dragon? What is she thinking?"

Another admiral said, "She will . . . she will detonate the capsule bomb on Dragon; everyone, stop her! Or we will lose the weapon."

"How?" Another admiral said through the hologram in their meeting room, "Shooting her is equal to destroying the capsule."

Then they agreed to shoot Lisa with a pulse bullets to disable the spacecraft's energy. When their shot would hit Lisa's plane, someone appeared in the space preventing it; he was the Prince himself, with a body of blue electricity that lit a fire, floating in space.

With a sound like thunder, so loud that many people heard it, the Prince said, "I'm Michael! I will not let you repeat the same mistakes; let us end what we started. This evil power will not be obtained by anyone. How big is a human being so he can be arrogant? They're like a grain of flakes in the ocean, and may The Creator still give mercy to pathetic little creatures like us."

Seeing Lisa's plane protected by the energy shield made by Michael, they panicked. Regardless, the spaceships from Central, UW, GaiGa and Star Ranger headed straight for Lisa to strike and block her path. Their ships and planes piled up and collided with each other even in such ample space, making the debris fly everywhere, destroying everything that was weak. Prince Michael then flew through the large spacecraft blocking Lisa's plane, so that their craft became a large hole. That terrible event was ignored by everyone; they wanted only to get the capsule to be able to use its strength — providing unlimited energy for their power.

"Don't let her use that weapon!" said an Admiral frantically.

He was Admiral James who was blocking Dragon from the rear, while Admiral Rasputin was in the front. Admiral James frantically directed the Mothership; it was a charge to hit Lisa. Their spacejet and Wingman were stopped by Michael, who hit their small space planes with intense lightning, destroying everything. He saw that James' Mothership, which was fifty kilometers long, was too big for him to beat, while Lisa was blocked by the giant ship filled with turrets.

"Finish this, complete what has finished us," Michael said, then directed all the energy from his body to protect Lisa's plane.

Lisa's plane flew into James's mothership, with the powerful energy shield that Michael gave between the planes; Lisa flew without stopping or crashing and broke through all the giant ships' layers. She passed the first wall, the second wall, entered the halls, runways, barracks, cities inside the ship, and continuously passed through the many things the mothership kept without stopping.

"Sir!" said a ship command operator. "Admiral James! The replica plane has entered our ship; she was in the inside of our ship without stopping."

"What? How could it be? Like a bullet that doesn't stop after penetrating our body — impossible," James said in surprise.

Lisa flew continuously without stopping, inside the ship's stomach, she hit many things, from the planes to the people inside.

Lisa thinks to herself, *Must, must be stopped, this is the only way that the Dragon won't kill anyone again.*

Then the last layer of the ship was pierced. Lisa saw the big Dragon in front being blocked by Admiral Rasputin. She saw the capsule she was carrying become unstable, and she knew that the time had come. A GaiGa mothership that is five times larger than James' mothership then intends hit her.

Felidean Admiral named FerXin said in human language to Admiral James, "Admiral, get out of there. All our sacrifices will be in vain if the weapon is destroyed there."

Quickly, James entered the spacejet in his command room and flew away from there. Suddenly, the James' mothership was broken in two pieces from the friction of the titanic mothership of the faction GaiGa. FerXin's mothership then flew towards Lisa and shot her with force shots that were rarely owned by UW ships. The Force shot destroyed the shield of Lisa's plane, and the plane stopped flying.

"Force shot? That is one of my works they stole," said Michael.

Then Michael flew towards the GaiGa mothership—he knew the weakness of the canon. Many automatic planes GaiGa sent out to find Michael tried to shoot him, but Michael absorbed the energy of their weapons and became stronger.

* * *

FerXin got angry and blew up his own planes which were chasing Michael. Michael shot energy from his hand on the tubes around the canon and destroyed them. Michael then gave a thrust of energy that exploded near Lisa's plane and made the flight fly forward quickly in a vacuum.

"Very good," said Michael "You have to do it, Lisa. I'm sorry and thank you."

Then Lisa saw the big Dragon in front of her, red and blue, like angry plasma energy. When the dragon was about to pass Rasputin's last defense, Lisa held both capsules.

Lisa said "Oh, what's the difference. After all, I already died a century ago."

Lisa then connected the two unbalanced capsules because they were too close to Dragon. When the power of Energy Zeal and Magnate Force were united, the power represents a quantum leap in great explosion, the power that everyone sought to sacrifice themselves. Nova started from Lisa's hand, like a big white light, like an angry star; the explosion was extraordinary and quick.

The space fleet was far away, then flew as far away as they could, but those who were too close tried to turn their ships and flee. FerXin, who saw it, was just silent.

A warrior came and asked, "FerXin, my lord. Why don't we fly away?"

FerXin said in a relaxed tone, "Our machine uses the same power, energy core and magnate force so it makes that power faster than light. We don't have enough time to recharge. This ship is too big and slow, our plane is too small and weak."

Before they destroyed in the light, an admiral who was near the explosion said to his men, "Starboys, welcome to into the quantum world. It's an honor to be flying with you. "

The white light then turned blackish blue like indigo. Majestic scenery that was terrible for anyone.

On the planet, all the droids that were controlled became statues without stakes; all the space people were panicking.

Nora said, "Hey, Marco, this is how it feels when you die."

"Oh no!" Marco said fearfully.

"Fear and courage, that's what everyone needs. Goodbye," Nora said.

"At least, I am still the richest single human being on the

planet," Marco said resignedly and jokingly.

When the light approached from the sky, destroying everything, including the Dragon which was abolished and its energy sucked away, Prince Michael appeared before them. He no longer had flesh, only electric light.

Michael said, "This hasn't ended yet."

Michael then surrounded them with light; they all fell into a coma. A large energy ball surrounded them. He took them on the journey of space and time. They disappeared with Michael. The Nova got bigger and destroyed the planet with incredible speed. Soon, the sun on the Apen star system became unstable and changed color. A dangerous weapon. The star slowly pulled all the celestial objects in the system and eats them because of the loss of holo-force that holds the astro lines of star system bound order. Everything then devoured the star. Only a portion of the ships escaped, while the others vanished in the empty sky; they died even before the sun went berserk.

The incident was heard to everyone else in the galaxy, and they then formed the council again. Because the weapons have been lost forever, the committee began to look for people to blame, because they have lost the lives of hundreds of millions of crew, and other losses of the machines, aircraft, and robots. Unlike GaiGa and Central who were loyal to their leaders, United Worlds was a combination of human colonies that needed scapegoats. Then the decision was made, and they began to imprison other board members. UW was weak for several years due to loss of morale, which weakened some of their space defenses. The incident became one of the worst in the history of UW, with only a few survivors.

CHAPTER 21

Many months later, Marco opened his eyes. He saw a wooden roof—he was in a poor cottage in a warm area. He tried to get out of bed and stand up but fell because he was no longer able to walk.

"Not enough time," someone said.

Marco then saw Monica Valdez cutting vegetables with Nora. Nora's left hand had been replaced with a robotic hand made from ironwood.

Very shocked, he can't talk nor move. Suddenly received a strange power, Marco could talk clearly and said in a loud voice, "Hey! Am I in heaven? What is this? Oh my goodness. At first, I wanted to cry, but this place is too beautiful, so I will cry while laughing."

"Finally, you wake up from a coma! I was tired of having to go back and forth to the city to take the stuff, I'm not your mother or something." Nora said irritably.

"Why are you so angry? We survived, oh . . . even then if all this is true, and not a trick from the lab. Wait, this is not a hologram and manipulation, right? This is the real world." Marco asked.

"Of course it is. And yes, I'm angry! Because you are no longer my darling . . . nah, just kidding," Nora said.

Monica then came to lift Marco and said "I don't know, so . . . before you ask, Michael has kept me alive, he saved me from a Phoenix attack, just like you, but he lost you at that time."

"Oh" Marco answered, "Where are we? Where is that old bastard? He asked."

Nora answered "We suddenly appeared here, I don't know how, it must be him! Michael was not here anymore; he was gone. Before that he said, 'There will be more evil power, greater than yesterday's, come for more power' So he prepared us for something. That happened, one half of a year ago."

"I've been in a coma for a half year? That's good; enough rest, I guess," Marco said.

Nora said again "We must continue to hide; you still have a little draong's electricity in your body, and we are on another planet far from the Apen star system. We are in the star system of the Garden Colonies in planet Big Nusa, a beautiful tropical planet terraformed for hundreds of years! Get out and look — all the palm trees, rainforest, blue ocean; everything is real and not a single plastic tree! The leaves its breathing!"

Marco then crawled out of curiosity; he saw wide white sand, palm trees, rainforest, light blue seas, bright blue sun, and futuristic cities in a distance. Marco hugged them; he saw a black ball that could speak.

"It is Alexa," Nora said, "I saved her from a Chasseur plane; we need a new body for her. I mean, new fighter plane, but think that is impossible for now."

Marco then said "I can still see the sadness in your eyes."

Nora replied "True, I have seen more death than anyone, the death of everyone on my planet, even my own death. But it's okay now, I have no hormones to feelings sad, only some weird scripts inside my body."

Soon, Marco and Monica were married there, and gave birth to a son while continuing to live on a remote island in the large and beautiful archipelago colonies; the planet was twice the size of the earth, controlled by UW with a population of fifty billion, and had many countries but was filled by wilds.

CHAPTER 22

The story doesn't end here; a few years later, in a distant star system, two new giant alien Primer Species emerged: Amphibian from the Kingdom of AzuRa Clan, originating from the Andromeda Galaxy; and Reptilian from the Kingdom of LaZaRa Clan, originating from the Triangulum Galaxy. They came with advanced technology, which had never been seen by humans from botengineering and bioengineering cutting-edge technology.

The Reptilian species of LaZaRa had a stature like a dark green scaly humanoid lizard that was not too rough. The Reptilian species had a head like a reptile, like a lizard combined with a cobra. The LaZaRa race had rare and robust hair. Their skin was hard and rough. They came in various sizes; their tails were also long; they were humanoid, with large nails, big tail and small canines. They were colored from dark yellow to dark green. They had statures like tailed humanoid lizards — scaly, glow-eyed, and head like a cunning snake.

AzuRa had an alien species called Amphibian, without hair where the female biological body was stronger, so that the Amphibian males were shorter and had ear screens next to the head which were amphibious respirators not like the bald female Amphibians. AzuRa females were taller in height, ranging from three to four meters or more, just like the height of the Valkyries of Neo-Human. Their muscular bodies were shaped with great abdominal muscles. Amphibians were built like humans but were two times as tall, and varied in color from light purple to indigo. They had human-like teeth, their skin was slippery in white oily like fish, and their big tongues were black and could be stuck out long like snakes. They had statures like tailless humanoid Amphibia—scaly, big dark-eyed, webbed fingers, and small noses.

There was a LaZaRa representative named KadeRa, green-eyed and dressed in horned metal—while the AzuRa representative, named MiSha'h, dressed in light purple cloth from thin clothes with a cape and hood, looked muscular in her abdominal muscles. They were greeted by the figure of GaiGa Clan named XiraGa, a furry Felidean male.

XiraGa welcomed the two while saying, "Greetings, my sisters. A new history is made today. My name is prince XiraGa from Planet Xanetari. Tell me what your goals are and what you need! We are the Felidean Clan ready to help the LaZaRa Clan and the AzuRa Clan."

* * *

KadeRa, one of LaZaRa's representatives said, "Clan? You guys are still ruled by the elders as we thought. I am KadeRa, and the name of the original planet I came from, I have forgotten. I was born in voids on a plane . . . "

XiraGa stopped KadeRa's conversation, "Sorry, what do you mean by still being ruled by the elders? What happened to your elders and, if not Clan, then what is your ruling system called."

MiSha'h, who was standing nearby, said, "First, the elder is our culprit of being sinful, so there is no reason to respect them; some of them were killed and others were imprisoned forever. Second, don't call it clan again, but Kingdom. You still hold on to the Intergalactic league, while, on the contrary, we have

212

arrived at the Multigalactic League. Another Kingdom Combination that was once a Clan in each Galaxy formed an Empire with one goal: to destroy the elders and form an alliance against invaders. Join us, and forget the elders who have made you suffer. Elders choose free will, which makes the dimensional kingdom. Our Creator left us to a free world with suffering because of our own devil mind, with dead and pain as lessons."

Hearing those words, XiraGa became afraid but did not believe; scared, he said, "You are traitors! All those words are lies; the Elder Watchers are guarding the galaxy, and you are heterodox! You are infidels!"

The two representatives laughed; then KadeRa said, "Attack us if you are brave enough. It makes no difference. Like your elders have hidden the history books for too long, it's time for your library to open and this galaxy to be saved from its own errors."

XiraGa and the people tried to retreat because it appeared that the two representatives were quite strong. MiSha'h took out a weapon formed of billions of small invisible Nanomachines that arose from the side then hardened; her left hand had a knife, and her right turned to a bow. The MiSha'h shot XiraGa's leg with a bright arrow that could reach its target through his armor. XiraGa fell before he could run away. While kneeling, MiSha'h leaned forward to cut off his head and said, "This blood, will be the beginning of salvation. Whoever believes, let his blood be saved from their error; who does not believe, let his blood spill into salvation for those who believe."

The GaiGa guard around it saw him while shouting, "Infidel! Infidel!" Then they fled by plane and were about to leave the place.

MiSha'h then read the code through her voice, the sound making an invisible Nano-sized machine, called chakra machine that wrapped her body. The chakra energy amounted to millions of small machine cells that were used to form various tools such as weapons, shields, poisons, respirators, and so on. Unlike shield energy from a galaxy that was quite primitive. MiSha'h's voice made a black purple flame around her hand; then with her arrow, she shot and burned the area. GaiGa's guard around her tried to shoot MiSha'h, but the Nano Chakra Cell around her body protected her. The fire burned quickly — a form of fire that was different from the one in the Milky Way Galaxy, burning purple to black and was not luminous.

KadeRa said "My sister, this is enough, we have shown them. Let's catch what is left of them."

A brown giant Marvel man or pure human who was there looked and was surprised. "Unbelievable to the eyes. What kind of fire is this? A fire that doesn't emit light? They must have come to bring many new things."

KadeRa responded while looking at the human, "We were also surprised by a variety of new things here, one, haired creature and the other was hairless in one galaxy."

They then began deploying various military colonies in different places in the Milky Way galaxy; their fleet was expected to reach the planet Nusa in a few decades, after many wars.

Most parts of Garden Colonies haven't been discovered yet, leaving the planet with plenty of mysterious, abandoned colonies and lurking creatures from the deep dark. Not like Apen were there's no native alien, Garden filled by beasts and Primer like Gnomen. That would lead to the next complicated and prolonged conflict in one of the galaxies. The sun is just dust in the galaxy, while galaxies are like dust in the sands that fill the worlds. Only a few galaxies are condemned and melted to death by the Dimensional Kingdom around the Virgo Supercluster. They are free to do their will, with unrestricted knowledge, and evil from powerful, arrogant rulers who have never been defeated and humiliated by their Creator. They are an example of living beings who are not worthy of living forever because of sinful actions in their never-ending evil hearts, creatures that become worthless among the vastness of the universe. Or are they really that worthless for their Master of the realm? Will the Master save them from their own mistakes?

ABOUT THE AUTHOR

R. J. Breemer is a creative person in his busy life—for years he has created small indie games, short stories, music, and comics. When became a science fiction novelist, he liked to write about strong characters in epic situations; space opera, futuristic thrillers, alien tales, monster stories, spiritual warfare, and more.